*Reading and Comprehension in the
African Context*

Zapf Chancery Policy on Peer-Reviewing

All scholarly and academic works published by Zapf Chancery are peer-reviewed by at least two scholars in the field to which the work belongs. The purpose of peer reviewing is to get a second opinion from the community of scholarship to which the author belongs and thus add value to the work. All peer-reviewing is "blind-reviewing," that is, the reviewer does not get to know the author, nor does the author get to know the reviewer.

Peer-reviewing is done with the help of a especially designed instrument awarding numerical score on originality (40%), quality and currency of the sources cited (20%), presentation (30%), and language & Style (10%). For a work to be published a minimum cumulative score of 60% on the British grading scale is required. Works falling below this score are referred back to authors for improvement and further reviewing until the desired score can be obtained.

****

Zapf Chancery Peer Reviewers (among others subject specific)

Prof Joseph Galgalo, PhD (Cantab.), Vice Chancellor and Associate Professor of Theology, St. Paul's University, Limuru, Kenya, Prof. Esther Mombo, PhD, DD (*HC*), Deputy Vice Chancellor (Academics) and Associate Professor of Church History and Gender Theology, St. Paul's University, Limuru, Kenya, Rev. CB Peter, BTh, BD, MTh, Senior Lecturer in Biblical Studies and Theology, St. Paul's University, Limuru, Kenya, Professor Chris L. Wanjala, Professor of Literature, University of Nairobi, Kenya, Dr. Godwin Siundu, PhD, Senior Lecturer in English and Literature, University of Nairobi, Kenya, Mr. Enoch Harun Opuka, BEd, MPhil, Development Education Pratitioner, Dr. John Blevins, ThD, Associate Professor of Research, Rollins School of Public Health, Emory University, Atlanta Georgia, USA.

Reading and Comprehension in the African Context

A Cognitive Enquiry

Agnes Wanja Kibui, MSC, Ph.D
Lecturer: Educational Communication
and Technology,
University of Nairobi

Zapf Chancery
Limuru, Kenya

First Published 2012
©Agnes Wanja Kibui and Zapf Chancery
All rights reserved.

Cover Concept and Design
C. B. Peter

Associate Designer and Typesetter
Nancy Njeri

Copyediting
C. B. Peter and Godwin Siundu, PhD

Editor and Publishing Consultant
C. B. Peter

Printed by
Kijabe Printing Press,
P. O. Box 40,
Kijabe.

Published by

This book has been printed on fully recyclable, environment-friendly paper.

Zapf Chancery Publishers Africa Ltd,
C/O St. Paul's University
P. O. Box Private Bag,
Limuru - 00217, Kenya.
Email: info@zapfchancery.org
Website: www.zapfchancery.org
Mobile: 0721-222 311

ISBN 978-9966-040-16-9

Foreword

This book makes an important contribution to existing knowledge on the processes of reading and comprehension by identifying the various approaches and corresponding theories. While most of us know the importance of the two processes, few of us have mastered the various cognitive theoretical approaches that can be adopted to make reading effective, informative and enjoyable. This book, well used, will definitely help us to reorient our perception of both reading and comprehension, as well as understand the various relevant approaches and theories.

The book is organized in various chapters that cumulatively lead to our entry into the three key areas. Chapter One provides important background to reading as a skill, explaining the hidden dynamics that avoid the process and outcome of reading. Chapter Two deals with comprehension and vocabulary, both very important aspects of the reading process, while Chapter Three focuses on the relationship between reading, remembering and perception. Chapters four and five deal with various ways of assessing comprehension and the role of the reader respectively. Ultimately, there is a very comprehensive bibliography that provides relevant information for any reader who may want to extend the reach of their knowledge in the area of reading as a process. A particularly commendable aspect of this book is the fact that the author has provided, through appendices, very helpful practical exercises in reading and comprehension. These exercises, if well undertaken, will no doubt sharpen the reading, comprehension and remembering skills of the learner, and at the same time allow the reader an opportunity to practice some of the theoretical pronouncements made by the author. This is especially so when viewed with the practical examples used in the chapters.

Also notable is the fact that while Dr. Kibui is dealing with complex linguistic concepts, the book is rendered in a language that is easily accessible even to a general reader. It is therefore a very valuable book to teachers, students and general readers who may have an interest in how reading works and how best to apply cognitive theory of reader and comprehension for better practice especially in African educational institutions.

Dr. Godwin Siundu
Senior Lecturer
Department of Literature
University of Nairobi

Preface

In writing this book, my aim has been to give an account of what it means to be a proficient reader. Proficient readers are people who can get the information that they want from a text efficiently. The topics I highlight have not been given much attention in recent reading text books. The skills needed for proficient reading have received little attention; hence, readers who have difficulty in reading and comprehension are not given extra remedial courses that could help them.

This book will be useful to those involved either directly or indirectly in education. In particular, this book could help teachers, educationalists and students in secondary schools and tertiary institutions. Even though the argument about the reading process and comprehension has not been over-simplified, I have tried to ensure that the language of my presentation remains simple and clear.

Agnes Kibui

Contents

Chapter One: Introduction	1
Background	1
A Kenyan Historical Perspective	2
Rationale for a Cognitive Study of Reading and Comprehension	8
An Overview of the Book	10
Chapter Two: Reading and Comprehension: An Overview	13
What Happens when We Read	13
Definitions of Reading	15
Approaches Taken by Readers in Reading	19
A Basic Theoretical Framework about Reading	21
Conclusion	25
Chapter Three: Reading and Comprehension: A Theoretical Framework	27
Comprehension and Vocabulary	27
Models of the Reading Process	30
The Bottom-Up and Top-Down (Interactive) Processes of Reading	31
The Cognitive Implications of Reading-Theories	40
Conclusion	43

Chapter Four: Reading and Comprehension: Cognitive
    Components   45
    Reading   45
    Memory   46
    Memory and Perception   47
    Memory and Words   48
    Memory and Comprehension   51
    Schema and Perception   54
    Vocabulary and Reading Performance   56
    Relationship between Knowledge of Word
        Meanings and Comprehension   58
    Word Meanings, Schema and Reading
        Comprehension   61
    Strategies for Reading   63
    Learning English as a Second Language   66
    Conclusion   71

Chapter Five: Reading and Comprehension:
    Techniques of Assessment   73
    Approaches of Reading Assessment   73
    The Informal Reading Inventory (IRI)   73
    The Oral Reading Miscue Analysis (ORMA)   75
    The Cloze Test   76
    Conclusion   80

Chapter Six: Reading and Comprehension: Some
    Practical Applications   81
    Extensive Reading   81
    Some Approaches for Teachers and
        Curriculum Developers   85
    The Teaching Process   88
    Teaching Vocabulary   89
    Proposals for Teachers as Examiners   91

Chapter Seven: Concluding Remarks 93

Appendices 93

Bibliography 115

Index 121

CHAPTER ONE

Introduction

Background

According to the 1999 National Population Census the Kenyan population is composed of Africans who belong to different mother tongues, Asians of several Asiatic languages, Europeans of different nationalities, Arabs and other nationalities that come from diverse linguistic backgrounds. The African languages are traditionally regarded as belonging to four major linguistic groups: Bantu (for example, Gikuyu, Akamba, Luhya), Para-Nilotic (for example, Nandi, Kipsigis, Maasai), Cushitic (for example, Orma, Somali, Galla), and Nilotic (for example, Luo). These tribes conceal basic information concerning the rich linguistic diversity that is characteristic of Kenya.

The Kenyan Government (1999) listed 42 African tribes who speak different languages. Besides these African languages, there is Kiswahili which is commonly associated with the coastal people. The Kiswahili language developed as a lingua franca between the early coastal traders notably, the Arabs and the indigenous coastal people. Since the vast majority of the coastal people belong to the Bantu linguistic group, the language borrowed many morphological structures from the Bantu languages. The word Swahili is derived from an Arabic word, Sahila, which means coast. It is a combination of the local language and Arabic. From the coastal area where it is still widely used, Kiswahili spread into the hinterland along the

Mombasa–Kisumu railway line after which it spread into the rural districts. Kiswahili is currently widely used in the urban areas and in some rural districts where people are linguistically heterogeneous. The subjects in the research project speak their respective mother tongues, (that is, Gikuyu, Kalenjin, Luhya and Kikamba) and they have acquired Kiswahili in and outside classrooms.

The acquisition of English is quite different from Kiswahili as it is learnt only in schools where it is taught as a subject which means that do not practice English after school because the language that is used in most homes is either Kiswahili or vernacular. Most of these learners do not stay in their homes to read in the evenings because there are no reading facilities at their homes. Instead, they hang out with their friends in the neighbourhood where they speak Pidgin English which is known as 'sheng'. This is a mixture of English, Kiswahili, and many local languages. According to Espelago (2001) peer pressure dictates that for one to belong and be accepted in a group, he must behave like it. Therefore, the Kenyan youth must speak 'sheng' as speaking English is unacceptable and is regarded as a formal way of communication. The speaking of 'sheng' hampers the development and mastery of English. Therefore, the environment at home does not assist these learners as they struggle to acquire and learn vocabulary.

A Kenyan Historical Perspective

The history of the establishment of Kenya, as an independent nation plays an important part in understanding the present situation of language use, policy and the attitude the Kenyan nationalities have towards English. During the colonial period, the colonial government discouraged the use of Kiswahili in the education system with some regarding its teaching to those who had received early education in other vernaculars as a "complete waste of time and effort" (Muthiani, 1984:12). Some Christian missionaries on the other hand distrusted it because of its Islamic connotations. The place of mother tongue teaching was largely undisputed because it was favoured as the initial medium of instruction by all the parties concerned.

The colonial government's wishes as expressed by the then Director of Education (Mr. Orr) was to make English the lingua franca of East Africa and in his words "that is the star to which we must hitch our wagon" (Muthiani, 1984:6). Speakers of English were favoured vis-à-vis those of other languages. Consequently, good jobs were the preserve of those who could speak English. As a result, many Kenyans saw the knowledge of English as a key to prestige, material benefits, and social status. They equated education with English. This attitude is still prominent in Kenya.

English as a medium of instruction plays a major role in Kenyan schools and institutions of higher learning making it crucial in determining the performance in other subjects. Success at primary, secondary and tertiary levels in terms of vocabulary and comprehension has been seen to depend on the level of achievement in the four skills relating to English (Waithaka, 1993).

The same observation has been made by Omutsani (1997: iii) as he states that one pitfall is the English/Literature syllabus in our secondary schools. With the advent of the 8-4-4 system of education, (that is, eight years in primary, four years in secondary, and four years in university) the Ministry of Education and the Kenya Institute of Education yoked English language to Literature in what has been described as 'the integration approach'. The corollary of this is that certain important teaching methods like discussion, drills, dramatization and others are discarded in favour of those that can expressly meet the purpose of covering the syllabus. In that event, learners fail to learn certain language skills.

Amisi (1997:4) highlights the same observation as he states that since the introduction of the integrated system of teaching English in Kenyan secondary schools, a lot seems to have been taken for granted by educationists and learners to the disadvantage of both learners and teachers. It is an open secret today that teachers have given up trying to control the use of mother tongue in schools. For young people today, the pride of being fluent in any one language is nonsensical and old fashioned. 'Sheng' is one of the greatest blows to efforts to teach young people how to speak and write good English.

Concern about low attainment levels of secondary school leavers has been constantly raised by the Ministry of Education, the Kenya National Examinations Council annual reports, and the public. For example, according to the K.N.E.C. report (1993) Muya had this to say: "Judging by some of the examination scripts that land in the council's rooms, one can say that some candidates are virtually illiterate as they hardly communicate" (Muya 1993:12); and Oyaya (2001:14): "The way English is taught in schools leaves a lot to be desired if the kind of letters employers receive is anything to go by. Most of school leavers are unable to construct intelligible sentences in a 300- word application letter." Part of the blame has been attributed to the teaching and learning of the English language. Comments such as, "if these pupils were not so poor in English they would have done better in history or chemistry" (Waithaka, 1993: 5) are common. This means that English is at the heart of every learning process in each of the subjects. Thus, teaching any subject means teaching language and cognitive processes.

Since Kenya's independence, a number of commissions and bodies of inquiries have been constituted and appointed to look into its education system. The commissions include: The Report of the National Committee on Educational Objectives and Policies (1976) and its findings known as 'The Gachathi Report', The Presidential Working Party on the second university (1981) and its findings known as "The Mackay Report'; The Report of the Presidential Working Party on Educational and Manpower Training for the next Decade and beyond (1988) known as the Kamunge Report; Report of the Commission of inquiry into the education system of Kenya (1999) known as 'Koech Report'. The report was called 'The Totally Integrated Quality Education and Training (TIQET).

The reports have all recommended the use of English as the medium of instruction from standard four.

The principle aim of these commissions has been relevant education to conform to the aspirations of the people and the national goals. They were also to design a type of education that would stimulate resourcefulness, a sense of dedication, and confidence which are essential elements as a whole.

It was the National Committee on Educational Objectives and Policies that recommended that the language of the school catchment area should be used as the prominent medium of instruction for the first three years of primary education. English should be taught as a subject from nursery school and become the medium of instruction from standard four. All the other reports have supported this recommendation.

The Presidential Working Party on the second University in Kenya recommended that the present changes in education be implemented in the 8-4-4 system of education. The system required the learners to spend eight years in primary school, four years in secondary and four years at university. The system was different from the former one in which learners spent seven years in primary school, four years in secondary education, two years in advanced secondary education, and three years at university. In January 1985, the Kenyan government launched the new system of education which, according to policy makers, has a technical and practical bias. These changes were to make the curriculum and general education system in Kenya more relevant and of immediate use to the learners.

The 8-4-4 system of education called for a new emphasis in the curriculum to achieve its aims. As such, English and Literature became a combined course which came to be known as the 'Integrated English Syllabus.' This syllabus included amongst others, topics on study skills which according to course designers "will be very useful for learners of English in tackling language and other subjects" (Kenya Institute of Education, 1987: ix). In the integrated English series, texts from other school subjects were incorporated. Learners were also required to learn study skills of note taking, note making, summarizing, scanning, skimming, interpretation of diagrams and charts amongst others.

After fourteen years of implementing the 8-4-4 system of education, the Koech Report (1999) suggested a revision of the curriculum with a view to trimming down some of the subjects' content and reducing the number of subjects that a student is expected to be examined on in the Kenya Certificate of Secondary Education (K.C.S.E.). The recommendation was made after complaints were raised by parents, teachers, and learners about overloading learners with assignments leaving them with very little time to study.

The reasons given for the overloading of the curriculum were the integration of various subjects which had made the content of the affected subjects too wide and rather unmanageable. Some of these subjects were the English language and Kiswahili. The report recommended that the existing integration be stopped and instead, the affected subjects be offered separately from secondary three to tertiary level.

To date (2012), the recommendations have not been implemented despite the many complaints that have been raised by the educators, curriculum designers and the general public about the decline in performance of the English language at K.C.S.E. examination. One of the major complaints from teachers and learners is that the English language syllabus is overloaded and that unless English and Literature are tested separately, complaints about the learners' poor performance in English will never abate.

Although Kiswahili is also a non-primary language to many Kenyans, the current language policy states that it should be introduced as a compulsory subject from kindergarten to form four as it is the national language in Kenya. There are many avenues and resources for learning Kiswahili so that the learner learning the language in schools has no problem in mastering it. On the other hand, the problem is very different for the same learner in his attempt to learn English. This is evidenced by the K.C.S.E. results of 2005 which were released on 1st of March, 2006. The results indicated that out of 260,665 candidates who did the examination, there were only 554 candidates who scored grade 'A' in English compared to 2,122 candidates who scored 'A' in Kiswahili (Aduda, 2006:2).

The teaching and learning of English is made difficult because the classroom is the only environment where the learner can hear and attempt to speak it. This is a general problem experienced by learners who learn English as a second language which has been observed by Gebhard, (2000) when he points out that in English as a second language settings there are fewer chances for students to apply what they study to communicative situations outside the classroom and that the only comprehensible English some of these learners hear and read is in the classroom. This is the situation with the learners in this study. There is limited exposure and reinforcement outside the classroom despite the fact that in Kenya, English assumes extra significance because it is the medium of instruction. Its significance is highlighted in the English syllabus (Kenya Institute of Education, 1985:1) which says "English is a service subject; consequently, fluency in all aspects of language will undoubtedly enable the learner to perform better in other subjects". That means English helps us to communicate competently in all fields of study. This is in line with the interactive approaches to language teaching and learning which proposes that learners learn best by using the language to communicate with other people as opposed to studying rules. But this is not the case. The present Kenyan system does not assist students as they struggle to acquire a high proficiency in English.

Merging of English and Literature in 1986 has had an adverse effect on both the teaching and learning of English and has led to poor performance in the Kenya Certificate of Secondary Education Examinations as the syllabus is not adequately covered. One of the reasons is that English lost some lessons in the time–table to Literature and Kiswahili, thus, making it difficult for the teachers to cover the syllabus efficiently and adequately. As a result, complaints have been raised about the declining standards of the English language. For example, Muya (1993) states that a general outcry has been expressed by educationists, potential employers, and ordinary citizens to the effect that most of the secondary school leavers and university graduates have often not been fully equipped with the basic skills in reading and writing. He adds that Japheth Kiptoon, a renowned educationist and one time vice chancellor, lamentably admitted that many graduates were almost illiterate and had problems in reading instructions and writing letters of application. In 1999 and 2002, the Kenya National Examinations Council indicated a significant drop in candidates' performance in English. On the basis of these comments, it is clear that the proficiency in English comprehension and vocabulary needs to be established in order to address the problem.

Rationale for a Cognitive Study of Reading and Comprehension

Hutchinson and Waters (1987), Storch and Whitehurst (2002) have summarized the educational objectives stated in terms of the expected performance of a learner in language and have thrown some light on the best ways to achieve the objectives. The cognitive and affective codes provide clear guidelines in terms of what is expected of the learner. The two codes are related because, before learners can actively think about something, they must want to think about it. The emotional reaction to the learning experience is the essential foundation for the initiation of the cognition process. That is, the way learning is perceived by the learner will affect the type of learning that will take place.

Some of the objectives defined in the Kenyan Certificate of Secondary Education English Syllabus require the learner to develop more confidence in his ability to express himself intelligibly in English (K.C.S.E. Syllabus 1989-1990:25). It states that at the end of the course the learner should be able to:
1. Develop more confidence in his ability to express himself intelligibly in English.
2. Listen and speak intelligibly and intelligently English in different situations.
3. Understand a passage by following its content, arguments and narrative sequence and be able to infer information, meanings, attitudes and intentions and present such information in a variety of ways.

The general objectives require the learners to develop a high level of language proficiency for their future educational or occupational purposes for which the English language will be required (K.C.S.E.). However, a number of educators indicate that some of these objectives have not been realized. For example, Kamau (1996) states that some teachers of other subjects were hostile to the teachers of English as the latter were seen to hinder good performance in other subjects due to the learners' poor command of English. In her study, she found that the English language teachers were reluctant to involve science teachers in language learning. This reluctance fails to address one of the requirements of the Kenya National Examinations Council regulations and syllabus (1997 and 2005) which states that one of the general objectives of English is to make effective use of English in the study of other subjects in the curriculum and in the development of further learning.

It is clear that a learner's ability to understand all the other subjects in the curriculum, apart from languages, and even his level of performance in the examinations will be greatly influenced by his mastery of the English language. As English is the medium of instruction in Kenya, the Kenya National Examinations Council regulation stipulates that every entry qualification must include a pass in English. For a learner to qualify for the competitive courses at the University, he must have a good grade in English as basic skills are required for study at the university. In addition, learners are required to be proficient in the four skills of language, namely, reading, writing, listening and speaking. Those whose command of English is low are handicapped. Furthermore, learners need to communicate with the members of the public in clear, correct and acceptable English.

Although great significance is attached to English in the country and in schools in particular, the learners' performance in the subject is poor in the National examinations especially over the last fifteen years. This observation is also highlighted by Miheso (2005) when he states that in the recent past, results in the English Examinations at K.C.S.E level have been showing a steady decline in performance. Many candidates fail to attain an average grade.

The Daily Nation (1991) points out that it is important to re-examine the extent to which the current public examinations provide a true reflection of the candidates' ability in the English language; how they focus upon testing the sub-skills which are crucial to effective communication, both in the spoken and the written modes. Hence, there is a need to teach learners English so that they can use it competently in different situations in their future careers and not only for examinations purposes. It is therefore necessary to encourage learners to appreciate the importance of English as a tool for fostering understanding of other subjects and to further effective development. The present study focuses on two sub-skills: comprehension and vocabulary as part of the written mode. The study takes into consideration that part of language learning means learning the vocabulary and acquiring competence in the use of the words so that one can understand and speak the language.

An Overview of the Book

This book is divided into seven chapters as follows:

Chapter One contains an introduction in which a brief background to the study was provided and the problem was stated. It also stated objectives of the study. The chapter also provides information on the methodology used to collect and analyze data. Attention was also given to literature regarding comprehension and vocabulary acquisition.

Chapter Two offers a theoretical overview of the cognitive processes of reading and comprehension. It also discusses the importance of reading including views about reading and approaches taken by readers. The chapter provides an outline of models of the reading process including bottom-up, top-down, and interactive process of reading.

In Chapter three, a theoretical framework for reading and comprehension has been set. The chapter also discusses the relationship between comprehension and vocabulary. An outline of the role of memory has been provided including memory and perception, memory and words, and memory and comprehension. The chapter also explains the importance of schemata in comprehension, especially in light of studies that have considered comprehension and vocabulary knowledge, including strategies for reading and the Kenyan learners. It also focuses on studies on English proficiency in Kenya, and assessment of comprehension.

Chapter four focuses on the major cognitive components of the processes of reading and comprehension, especially, memory, perception, and vocabulary.

Chapter five provide a brief introduction of some major techniques of the assessing the efficacy of reading and comprehension.

Chapter six attempts to wrap up the hitherto discussed theoretical considerations into some practical applications and applied guidelines to help teachers to obtain better practice within their institutional professional contexts.

Finally, Chapter seven offers some concluding remarks on the entire project

CHAPTER TWO

Reading and Comprehension: An Overview

What Happens When We Read

The ability to read with understanding is a skill that is essential in modern society as there is a lot of material that needs to be read and understood. Yet, a large number of people never master it completely. Readers go unprotected from the struggle with job application forms, and insurance policies, recipes, and advertisements; and they also miss much of the joy of reading for pleasure. In a literate society, skill in reading is imperative since so much of what one needs to know is communicated via written text. For example, instructions on how to perform a task, or find out directions, instructions on how to operate machines, precautions one needs to take when trying a new drug or ointment. This indicates that it is not possible to function in modern society without reading.

Most learners rely on their reading ability in order to gain information or expand their knowledge. Learners' proficiency in reading is essential since most of their learning of all subjects is available to them in written text and is processed to them through reading. For learners who are learning English as a second language, reading skill is of great importance since in most cases it is the only readily available exposure to the target language which might not be spoken outside the classroom. That means that in order to retain some of the knowledge gained in a course of study, the learner of a second language must continue to read in that language for many years after graduating from the course.

Reading is interactive in nature. It is viewed as an interaction between the reader, the author and the text. This interaction is defined in terms of the relationship between the reader, the text and the context in which the reading act is being preferred. The reading process inherently involves the interaction of a reader and a text. The reader is considered to be a language user and the text is considered to be an instance of language in use. The implication here is that if readers are proficient in the language, they will be capable of ascribing meaning to and interpreting meaning from the text. When a person reads the text, she or he responds not only to the meaning expressed in the linguistic elements, but also takes into account the socio-cultural context which is reconstituted through the language patterns.

Thus, it can be concluded that the ability to comprehend depends on a variety of factors. These are factors within the reader, which have been shown to have an effect on reading process and the product of reading. There are also aspects of texts to be read and which could contribute to the reading process. The interaction aspects within the reader and that of the text give an overall picture on the act of reading.

Aspects within the reader include the state of the reader's knowledge, the reader's motivation to read and the way this interacts with the reasons why the reader is reading. It also includes the strategies readers use when processing the text, other reader variables like sex, age and personality are important aspects within the reader. Aspects of the text that might facilitate, or make difficult the reading process include text content, text organization, sentence structure, layout, the relationship, verbal and non-verbal text, and the medium in which the text is presented.

The role of the reader and the specific use of the context within this relationship are important if we have to understand how reading comprehension is achieved. It is within this model that background knowledge or prior knowledge of the reader plays a great role in the reading process.

Definitions of Reading

Linguists categorize reading into three capacities: reading as saying, reading as understanding, and reading as thinking (reflective). In the contemporary parlance of reading, these three fundamental competencies are referred to as decoding, comprehension and response.

In general language, the term decoding implies understanding. In reading, the term generally means converting printed language to spoken language whether it is understood or not, and whether it is converted overt (oral speech) or to covert (inner speech). In decoding, the reader produces the spoken analog of the printed language but not necessarily the thought analog. Another preferable term is recording, implying that the code has changed from orthographic print code to phonological speech code. Decoding at word level implies assigning a meaning as well as pronunciation to a printed word.

Comprehension is the essence of reading. It is the thinking we do to interpret the meaning in text. Whereas decoding involves producing a spoken analog of printed language, comprehension involves producing a thought analog of printed language. Comprehension is the reconstruction of the author's message: the author constructs a message and encodes in it printed language, and the reader decodes the printed language and reconstructs the meaning. Comprehension is central to reading as it occupies the central place on the continuum where input from the print and input from the reader are in central balance.

Response, the third fundamental competency of reading, involves a personal reaction to what is read, the contemplation of the ideas and feelings evoked by the text, responding to the text both cognitively and affectively. This competency involves reading beyond the lines, going beyond literal statements and inferential probability to finding personal relevance and significance.

Many scholars in their attempt to understand how reading is learnt have come up with different definitions of what reading is. The proposed definitions vary according to the views the scholars hold of what it means to read.

Weaver (2002) and Smith (1997) explain that learners' concepts of reading often reflect the kind of instruction they have received. Thus, if the teacher spends a lot of time teaching correspondences between letters and sounds, the learners will conclude that reading means pronouncing letters and sounding out words. If the teacher spends a lot of time reading text to and with learners and discussing the meanings with them, the students will conclude that reading means getting meanings from the text. Whatever the instructional approach, it is likely to affect the children's implicit definitions of reading and hence, their strategies for dealing with written text.

Reading has been defined as a form of problem solving. This means that meaning resides in the intentional, problem solving and the thinking processes of the reader as the reader participates in the interchange with a text. Reading, thus, is an act of communication in which information is transferred from a transmitter (writer) to a receiver (reader). Such information is transmitted as a form of meditative thought; a form of decoding graphic symbols to speech and processing the resulting language. In summary, reading and comprehension means identifying words by learning letter-sound relationships first and then decoding words letter-by-letter. It also means constructing meaning, and using everything the reader knows in order to do it.

Reading is partly a verbal process interrelated with thinking and all the other communication abilities—listening, speaking, and writing. Specifically, it is the process of reconstructing from printed patterns, the ideas, and information intended by the author. It is somewhat like the process of listening to people and reconstructing their ideas from sound patterns. Learning to read develops from learning to use and understand oral and written language. Learning to read fluently requires applying existing thinking strategies to written ideas; hence, the cultivation of the cognitive learning process is integral to any program to develop the reading process.

Reading is not necessarily a verbal process in the sense of a phonological act, unless, as in the case of a beginner each word is said out loud as the learner monitors his or her own reading. At times, learners read difficult passages aloud, or even whisper them in order to attain maximum understanding. Silent and speed reading may require inner speech, but the actual pronunciation of words is glossed over. The skilled reader does not need complete phonological or syntactic information to comprehend what he is reading. The definitions of reading supplied by Hittleman (1983), Weaver (2002), and Block (2004) include the activity of thought-choosing, judging, valuing, and communication, that is, the grasping of the writer's intent, whether it be factual or fiction, ideas or feelings. It is a two way interaction between a reader and a writer. In addition, reading is also a personal affair as readers have their own intentions and motivations for reading.

Since there are several definitions of reading, it is clear that it can not be defined in a single term as it is a process that involves the reader, (his or her goals and tools, which are reading strategies), the text, and the author. Therefore, in order to understand reading, one has to consider the factors that influence the role of each of these elements in the reading process, that is, the context in which the text is written and read. For example, the format in which the text is written and organized has to be considered in order to know the purpose of the text. The writer and the reader have to share some understanding in order for the text to make sense to the reader.

In an attempt to obtain meaning from what the author is expressing in the text during the reading process, the reader is helped by his or her own specific purpose for reading, interest in the text, language, and strategy use, knowledge and experiences. In addition, the text with its features such as organization, type of text, content, general and main ideas, sentence structure, and vocabulary, lends itself to understanding by the reader who engages with the author in the reading process by trying to understand the text. This interaction involves an exchange of ideas between the reader and the author that is represented in the text. The author attempts to make sense of the content in the text while the reader tries to understand what the author is trying to communicate. The text in the middle is like a tool through which these two people can understand each other. In order for the reader and the author to understand each other, the text should be comprehensible to the reader. Thus, reading is a give and take activity which Louise Rosenblatt (1978) calls a transaction.

Rosenblatt noted that since reading is a transaction between an author and a reader each reading experience is different. This is the theory that underlies the need for a wide variety of books in programmes for readers since many books have more than one possible interpretation. Seeing reading as transaction with texts foregrounds reading as dynamic and organic in character, as well as acknowledging that readers bring previous knowledge, beliefs and attitudes to the reading process. It is an active process of negotiating meaning between the writer of the text and a reader. The writer interacts with the reader by trying to anticipate how an imagined reader may react to what he or she is writing. When the text is eventually read, the reader has to negotiate the meaning of the text by trying to reconstruct the writer's ideas as they were intended. Secondly, Rosenblatt posited that there are two ways that people read depending on the nature and purpose of the text as well as the reader's purpose. They can read to find out information, which is called efferent reading, and they can read for enjoyment, which is called aesthetic reading.

The meaning of the text can arise from this transaction. The reader is the person seeking to make meaning by transacting with a text, of whatever kind. The author of a text is making meaning via that text, and in this sense, meaning resides in the text. The reader and the text interact in the creation of meaning. Through it, a reader is able to understand and interpret written information. When the writer and the reader share a lot of the same knowledge and experience, there will be a lot of overlap between their individual schemes. When they have had very different experiences, there will be less or no overlap. As a result, this makes transaction of meaning more difficult as the reader has to work extremely hard to alter her or his existing schemata so as to include experiences and ideas from the text, and to make meaningful sense of those ideas.

Quite often, comprehension is difficult for second language readers because of cultural factors. For example, a study by Parry (1987) in Gebhard (1999) shows that failure by Nigerian learners to achieve high scores in the English language section of the West African School Certificate Examination was due in a large part to two cultural factors. First, the West African physical and social environment of the learners is very different from that reflected in European-influenced passages in the English reading section of the examination. Second, the act of reading itself is cultural, as the Nigerian learners live in an oral culture where complex thoughts and ideas are remembered and expressed orally.

Learning depends on efficient comprehension of the text which is read. While this is important for all learners, it becomes a crucial point for most second language learners who lack a good command of the language.

Approaches Taken by Readers in Reading

Reading research has recognized several different approaches that can be taken by readers: Bottom–up, Top–down, and Interactive approaches to reading. In bottom-up approach, readers begin with the printed word, recognize words and decode meaning. In this traditional view, the reader is perceived as a passive decoder of sequential graphic-phonic-syntactic-semantic systems. According to this view, to be a good reader, one has to master these 'lower order' skills before proceeding to 'higher order' skills.

The view does not therefore accommodate reading skills such as critical thinking. It involves the acquisition of discreet reading skills, which may have limited value for the above mentioned purposes of reading. Educationists and learners are not merely concerned with the acquisition of discreet skills but with the development of a means to extend thought, learning, and independence as well as aesthetic experience. Therefore, the traditional view of reading is considered narrow in its application for the purposes of learning to read because in this view, the readers' grasp of vocabulary might remain at literal level, and their comprehension stunted. It limits the ability of readers to infer meanings, make predictions, make connections between cause and effects, draw conclusions, and test hypotheses.

The second approach shifts the emphasis of reading as a perceptual skill to viewing reading in a language context. This modern view starts with larger units of meaning. This view which is derived from the schema theory[1] stresses the centrality of the reader's prior knowledge and accounts for the acquisition of knowledge and the interpretation of the text through the acquisition of schemata: networks of information stored in the brain which act as filter for incoming information. If these schemata are relevant, reading is said to be successful. Recent studies have questioned bottom-up and top-down approaches as adequate descriptions of the reading process. Grabe's (1991) mode incorporates feedback mechanism that allows knowledge sources to interact with visual input. Stanovich (1986) has developed an interactive compensatory model in which 'higher-up' or 'lower-down' components of reading process interact. Examined against this interactive view, reading is considered as a whole process and cannot be divided up into sub-skills or separate units. Readers are not passive identifiers of letters and words but active contractors of their own knowledge.

Implicit in the interactive view is that good readers are not only rapid in word recognition but are precise as well. Good readers

---

[1]Schema theory was developed by R. C. Anderson, a respected educational psychologist. This learning theory views organized knowledge as an elaborate network of abstract mental structures which represent one's understanding of the world. The term schema was first used by Piaget in 1926, so it was not an entirely new concept. Anderson, however, expanded the meaning. http://www.sil.org/lingualinks/literacy/implementaliteracyprogram/schematheoryoflearning.htm. Accessed 05 July 2012.

are able to inspect what they read and also note various aspects of the text. They take in letter features of short words simultaneously and appear to recognize all the letters in a word. The ability to recognize words rapidly and accurately is an important predicator of reading ability in the first and second language reading.

Another concept underlying the interactive view of reading is that the reader is the main player in the interaction. Readers bring to the text all their years of experience, all their prior knowledge about how the world works, memory of other texts encountered, and all their social and cultural expectations and assumptions about the texts in question and the authors. Other players in this interaction include the authors of the text who bring in their ideas and all their social and cultural expectations and assumptions about the texts and their readers, peers, and teachers.

The context in which the act of reading takes place is seen as playing a part in this interactive view of reading. Context sets constraints. It may influence motivation depending on how the content matter to the reader takes place or for what purpose the reading takes place. The way learners read is determined by the tasks they are asked to perform, and their motivation to read. Thus, the context within which the reading act takes place determines the nature and quality of comprehension. Through this whole view of the reading process, reading is seen first, as a language process and therefore as an act of communication. Second, reading is a cognitive process and therefore, readers have to create meaning from the text. Third, reading is a social process and therefore, readers have to appropriate the meaning of the text through various social interactions. As they do this, they share a cultural identity.

A Basic Theoretical Framework about Reading

Vygotsky's (1978) social cultural theory proposes that learning occurs through a social interaction with a more knowledgeable person, who in this case is the teacher. The more knowledgeable person provides the right amount of support to help the learner to the next level of understanding. In order to provide the appropriate amount of support in book experiences, teachers determine the level of understanding and engagement of the learner.

Mulcia and Olshtain (2000), and Unsworth (2000) explain that in the 1990s, new literacy approaches have evolved which support Vygotsky's social cultural view. These can be viewed within the social literate school of thought which views reading as a social and cultural event involving written language. According to this approach to reading, the reader constructs the meaning of the text within a culture. Reading is therefore viewed as a social process focusing on author-reader interaction.

Content schemata organize implicit cultural knowledge and background knowledge to the content of the text and because cultural knowledge is often implicit, texts based on a learner's culture are generally easier to process than other texts of a similar syntactic level. That is, a text of a known topic is better remembered by ESL(English as a Second Language) learners than a comparable text of an unknown topic.

Students in lower classes achieve less well in reading than students in middle classes. Such students may not have any innate reading problems; the problem is one of cultural difference. Where there is a large mismatch between the culture of the home and the culture of the school, learners experience difficulties in the school environment. That is, the types of reading materials and tasks such learners encounter presume middle-class orientations, language values, and processes. This disadvantages the lower class learners because, in school, the language used is that of powerful middle class discourse since the authors and the teachers belong to that class. This is the problem encountered by second language learners because they come from diverse backgrounds and ethnic groups.

Melink (1972) characterizes reading as reasoning. He argues that reading is a dynamic process, an elaborate procedure, weighing and organizing of elements, a selection of relevancies and the co-operation of many forces to determine final response. Melink's view of reading as reasoning has had much influence on subsequent conception of what reading is. Later views of reading amount to

agreeing or disagreeing with reading as reasoning. Those who view the essence of reading is transformation of graphemes to phonemes disagree with Melink's position, but those who hold the view that reading involves comprehension of what is read are in general agreement with his position.
The following are six aspects of the reading process:

1. Word recognition
2. Association of meaning with individual printed symbols
3. Literal comprehension
4. Interpretation
5. Evaluation
6. Assimilation

In this view, word recognition involves the ability to translate the written symbol into a spoken symbol. The reader uses the following clues to identify unknown words:

i **Context Clues**: these are clues embedded in text that helps readers to decide unknown words
ii **Phonic Analysis:** which is a process of using letters and letter sound to sound out and decode an unknown word
iii **Structural Clues:** a process involved in using prefixes, suffixed inflectional endings and root words to identify words and decode their meanings
iv **Dictionary:** is used to determine word meanings. The total process further involves the association of meaning with printed symbols
v **Literal Comprehension:** involves reading for central ideas and noting the way details are organized around these central ideas
vi **Interpretation:** this takes the reader beyond the printed text by requiring that the reader put together ideas which the author has not overtly related to one another and by requiring him to see the connection between what s/he is reading and her/his

past reading and experiences. As a result, the reader is able to make inferences and draw conclusions

vii **Evaluation:** requires the reader to make judgment rooted in what she/he has read; sort facts from opinions and evaluate the logic of the reasoning represented in the material she/he has read

viii **Assimilation:** involves the process through which the reader makes use of her/his reading

Thus reading components can be categorized under four headings as follows:

1. Word perception including pronunciation and meaning.
2. Comprehension, which includes a clear grasp of what is read.
3. Reaction to and evaluation of ideas which the text presents.
4. Assimilation of what is read, through fusion of old ideas and information obtained through reading.

This categorization attempts to incorporate three broad, but related views of reading. The view that equates reading to a process of recognizing printed words; the view that implies that reading involves recognition of elements of meaning or comprehension of the written symbols; and the important elements of meaning and reflection on their significances and critical evaluation.

Reading researchers and theorists have attempted to identify reading skills and sub-skills as follows:
1. Recalling word meaning
2. Drawing inferences about meaning of a word in context
3. Finding answers to questions answered explicitly or in paraphrase
4. Weaving together ideas in content
5. Drawing inferences from the content
6. Recognizing a writer's purpose, attitude, tone and mood
7. Identifying a writer's technique

8. Following the structure of a passage

Lists of skills and sub-skills have been criticized; firstly because they are not derived from the results of empirical observation; secondly, they are ill defined and give misleading impression of being discreet when they overlap. Thirdly, it is frequently difficult to get experts to agree on the skills which are examined by different test items. Finally, analysis of test performance does not illuminate the skills as discrete, separate entities within authentic reading contexts.

Conclusion
In this chapter I have tried to summarize the general process of reading and comprehension as a cognitive phenomenon. This means that meaning of the text is not naturally embodied in the text as assigned to it by the reader but (meaning) emerges from his particular response to various cultural and existential contexts.

The next chapter deals with the role played by vocabulary knowledge in the process of reading and comprehension.

CHAPTER THREE

Reading and Comprehension: A Theoretical Framework

Comprehension and Vocabulary

When reading, the ability to recognize as many words as possible is important. No reading comprehension can take place without the immediate recognition of the words in the text. A lack of knowledge of words in a text could lead to frustration and unwillingness to read further as it could hinder the automatic cognition processing which is caused by fluency in the language in which the learner reads. In order to process words mentally immediately, one needs automaticity, that is automatic word recognition. If there is no automaticity, or if readers take time to process the words mentally, then, comprehension has no time to happen and sometimes does not happen at all. Consequently, readers have to be fluent in the second language for comprehension to take place.

Reading makes an extensive use of short-term memory stores. For example, the comprehension of sentences with complex structures depends not only on understanding the structure itself, but also on the ability to store the bits of structure until they can be put together. Furthermore, if the immediately preceding text can not be remembered, it may be difficult to link together the information from different sentences and to work out the overall message carried by a text. Short term memory limitation could therefore be a source of comprehension problems. While this is a problem to first language readers, it is a major task to readers with English as a Second Language (ESL). Memory is important for word recognition as well as in comprehension of text, but children remember facts and words better if they are ordered into a story. Goetz and Armbruster (1980) report on research by Poulson, Kintsch and Premack (1979) in which they presented 15-18 logically or randomly ordered pictures depicting a story to 4-6 year olds. After viewing the complete set, the children were asked to describe the pictures one at a time. These children, particularly the 6 year olds, added story propositions to both the logically ordered as well as the randomly ordered pictures in an attempt to interpret them. After this, they were asked to recall the story without the pictures. It was found that children recalled those descriptions best that had been integrated into the text.

A study by Campbell and Sais (1995) support this hypothesis. They tested monolingual (English) and bilingual (Italian/English) pre-schoolers and found significantly higher performance by the bilingual students on many of the phonological and semantic tasks. Although both cohorts performed equally on picture-vocabulary and letter recognition tests, the bilingual children were superior on a test requiring them to sort pictures of objects by category according to the sequence of the story. This indicates that children have knowledge of logical relationships and the structures underlying simple stories that greatly influence their comprehension and memory of words.

In another study on the relationship between word recognition and comprehension, Perfetti and Hogaboam (1975); Perfetti and Lesgold (1979) found that skilled comprehenders are more rapid at oral word decoding than are less skilled comprehenders. This could indicate that skilled readers are able to use their skills in reading for meaning rather than for word recognition. Reading for meaning according to them depends upon vocabulary knowledge, short-term memory, syntactic integration, inferences, and other higher order overlapping skills that make demands on the same mechanism responsible for converting the printed code into the language code. Therefore, as skilled readers take less time to figure out meanings of unfamiliar words, they create more space for other reading skills such as prediction, understanding the meaning in context, anticipating language structures and responding to the message through interpretation.

Essential development in learning to read is the recognition skills that are impenetrable to factors such as knowledge and expectation. This allows the developing reader to recognize words while utilizing little processing capacity, and provides the comprehension processes with the raw materials required to operate efficiently.

Developing readers increase the number of words that they can recognize automatically, to a large extent, by repeatedly applying decoding rules to unknown letter strings. In this way, the application of decoding rules to unknown letter strings act as a self–teaching mechanism that increases the corpus of words that can be recognized automatically. Thus, decoding skills play a crucial role in the acquisition of automatic word recognition skills in developing readers. Consequently, word recognition aids comprehension skill of the text. Once readers recognize the words, they go directly to the meaning of the passage they are reading. Non-recognition of words slows down the reading speed and thus comprehension becomes minimal. As the reader hesitates and tries to remember the word or to analyze it by some means such as phonic, the information prior to the word is lost requiring him/her to begin again in order to preserve continuity. This usually happens very often with second language learners.

Weaver (2002) maintains that readers do not just add together the meanings of individual words in a sentence in order to get the meaning of the whole. A reader can not know what a word means until he sees it in a context as words have several meanings. In isolation, words have only potential meanings, that is, a range of meanings that a dictionary attempts to characterize. For example, Weaver gives the following examples of the word 'run':

a) Can you run the store for an hour?
b) Can you run the word processor?

c) Can you run the 500-yard dash?
d) Can you run in the next election?
e) Can you run in the next year's marathon?
f) I helped Samuel with his milk run.
g) They'll print 5000 copies in the first run.
h) Sherry has a run in her hose.
i) There was a run on snow shovels yesterday morning.
j) It was a long run.
(Weaver, 2002: 15-16)

Our mental schemas help us to understand the context. If we do not have mental schemas, we would not make practical use of the other kinds of context mentioned. For example, if we did not have an intuitive sense of grammar, we could not use grammatical context to limit a word's possible meanings to those that are appropriate for the verb (as in examples a through e) or to limit the word's possible meanings to those that are appropriate to the non function (as in examples f through j). This process of grammatically delimiting a word's possible meaning is so automatic that we are not often aware of it, but it nevertheless occurs and is made possible by our grammatical schemas.

Second language learners would not understand some of the above idiomatic expressions of the word 'run', because they relate to cultural practice and understanding. It is only when the word is used in the context that one or more of these meanings are actualized. Such learners depend on dictionaries for arriving at meanings that are not evident to them from the context itself. As a result, they take more time to figure out meanings of words so that there is less time left for other reading skills such as prediction, inference, evaluation, and so on.

Models of the Reading Process

In order to devise an assessment procedure for efficient reading and to derive meaning in context, we must know what it means to read a text and to understand it. A theory of reading must of necessity be a theory of comprehension. There is a difference between the process of reading and the result of that process. The process is the interaction between a reader and the text. The process is dynamic and different for the same reader on the same text at different times and with a different purpose in reading. There can be no single model of reading: "there are as many reading processes as there are people who read, things to read, and goals to be served. The purpose of reading is determined by the reader and the text to be read. For example, people will read carefully to a set of directions in order to try to understand them fully. In other contexts, the purpose for reading a text is more indeterminate. For example, people could have very different purposes for reading a text on a church sermon: to evaluate if the views correspond to their own or to obtain information for a lecture they are about to present or for enjoyment. Therefore, the purpose readers establish for reading a text will influence both what they read and how they read it.

The Bottom-Up and Top-Down (Interactive) Processes of Reading

Cognitive psychologists and psycholinguists have planned models of reading in an attempt to explain how the reader obtains meaning from print. Most of these models may be placed in one of the following categories: Bottom-up, Top-down, and Interactive.

LaBerge and Samuels (1976) formulated their model on the bases of automaticity in fluent reading, postulating a theory of 'automatic information processing'. This model takes the bottom-up view of reading. That is, the text defines the act of reading.

According to the bottom-up model, readers build understanding by starting with the smallest units of the message: individual sounds or phonemes. These are then combined into words, which in turn, together make up phrases, clauses, and sentences. After this, individual sentences combine to create ideas and concepts and relationships between them. According to this model, the different types of knowledge which are necessary in the reading process are applied in a serial, hierarchical fashion.

The model begins with the visual perception in which the reader analyses the information from the text by detectors which note the features such as lines, angles, intersections as well as the relational features such as left, right, up and down. These lead to the discovery of letter codes, spelling pattern codes, word codes, and finally to word group codes.

The next stage of the model deals with the phonological system where automaticity is achieved through practice in reading the syllabic components of the word. Sometimes, readers pronounce the word silently to themselves as they read in order to understand its meaning from the sound. The third stage of the model is the semantic system. After the reader has seen and heard the word, it is assumed that the meaning of the word can be elicited by means of a direct association between the sound of the word and its meaning. At first, the meaning is coded in memory but after some practice, the word becomes meaningful after it is heard. Here, the authors allow for the association between the phonological form of the word and its meaning to go in the other direction so that activation of a meaning unit could automatically stimulate a phonological unit.

LaBerge and Samuels (1976) view the reading process basically as translating, decoding or encoding process. The reader starts with letters and as he or she attends to them, begins to anticipate the words they spell. As words are identified they are decoded to inner speech from which the reader derives meaning in the same way as in listening. Reading comprehension is believed to be an automatic outcome of accurate word recognition. In bottom-up approaches, the reader begins with the printed word, recognizes the graphic stimuli, decodes them to sound, recognizes words and decodes meaning. Each component involves sub-processes that take place independently of each other and builds upon prior sub-processes but sub-process higher up the chain cannot give a feedback.

LaBerge and Samuels (1976) argue that it is important for young readers to be proficient in phonetic decoding and word recognition to facilitate comprehension. They emphasize the role of first understanding the words singularly as they occur and then moving from decoding of the word to comprehension. In their model, the reader perceives individual letters and words and transforms them to phonemic codes and moves on to the final comprehension of text. Emphasis is on the view that lower process such as word recognition must be 'atomized' without the reader's attention or consciousness.

In other words, LaBerg and Samuel's model involves four processing mechanisms: phonological, orthographic, meaning, and context. As the visual image of a string of letters is being processed, excitatory stimulation is sent to corresponding units in the phonological processor. If the letter string is pronounceable, the phonological processor will then send excitatory stimulation back to the orthographic processor. Thus, the activation of a word's meaning results in the excitation of the phonological units underlying its pronunciation. Consequently, the activation of its pronunciation automatically arouses its meaning. These connections make reading and learning to read possible.

With practice, processing normally becomes automatic and words are recognized through modularity. Modular processes occur rapidly and without the individual's attention and are influenced by prior knowledge structures stored in long–term memory. Since the modular processes are encapsulated, efficient word recognition skills operate independently of context. As a result, readers can concentrate on the message of the printed text. In order to read efficiently and understand, the model suggests that the reader must have a good knowledge of a language: spelling, syntax, semantics, and the informal flow of discourse.

Reading involves learning facts about the distribution of letter patterns in the language and the correspondences between spelling and pronunciation. This knowledge can be represented in terms of weights on connections in a distributed memory network that consists of simple processing units. Experience modifies the weights in reading and pronouncing words. The accuracy and speed of written word recognition depend mainly on the reader's familiarity with the word print. The more frequently a spelling pattern has been processed, the stronger, more focused, and faster will be its connections to and from the meaning processor. The more frequently a spelling pattern has been mapped onto a particular pronunciation, the stronger, the more focused, and faster will be its connection to and from the phonological processor. When a reader comes across less familiar words, the presence of the circular connectivity of all the processors serves in quickly obtaining likely responses.

Reading depends first on visual processing. The output of the orthographic processor depends on the speed and accuracy with which the individual letters are perceived as well as on the familiarity of the spelling patterns comprising the word. The meaning processor in turn depends on the quality and completeness of the orthographic and the phonological processors. If a word is highly predictable from the text, then, little orthographic and phonological information is needed. A proficient reader frequently moves directly from orthographic to the meaning processor.

Reading is not a simple process of decoding a text letter by letter, word by word, clause by clause, and sentence by sentence. Rather, it involves sampling the text, forming hypotheses about what it says, and then confirming or rejecting them. Fluent readers do not process words letter-by-letter. Just as readers do not comprehend sentences merely by combining meanings of individual words, they also do not perceive words merely by combining individual letters.

Readers do not identify all the letters in a word before identifying the word, even if the word occurs in isolation. Proficient readers when they perceive all the letters may be determining the letters after they have identified the word. That means, fluent readers do not have to read every word in a sentence; familiarity with structures, prediction, experiences, expectations, and so on allows readers to gloss over words that do not have a high meaning content. Even if readers perceive most of the letters in most of the words, it does not mean that most of the letters are perceived separately before the word is perceived. When we read for comprehension, we do not first identify the smallest units of language, letters, and then work upwards. Reading according to this view is a top-down process, involving activation of the reader's existing knowledge (schemata).

Top-down approaches view the interpretation process as a continuum of changing hypothesis about the incoming information. Smith (1971, 1988, and 1994) and Goodman (1968, 1976) are major proponents of such an approach. They emphasize the use of previous knowledge in processing a text rather than relying upon individual sounds (phonemes) and words. They have the belief that readers who are unable to identify segmented sounds in isolation from the words they form a part of, are quite able to identify segmented words so long as they are presented with the surrounding context. For example, when presented with the phoneme \hi/, it is not possible to predict which phoneme follows it. But if presented with the phoneme in a context such as 'the boy \hi/ the dog', it is easy to predict that the following sound or letter is likely to be \t/. This suggests that readers rely on more than just the sound signal to decode a written message; they rely on the prior contextual knowledge as well.

Readers find it easy to read new words by analogy with the parts of words they already know in print. This can be supported by a study done by Moustafa (1995) cited in Weaver (2002). Moustafa wanted to know which would be more helpful when emergent readers tried to read unfamiliar print words: their knowledge of individual letter-sound correspondences, or their prior ability to recognize one-syllable words with the same rhyme. She asked the children to read certain nonsense words or words they usually would not know in print, but only after she had determined the extent and nature of their letter-sound knowledge and their ability to read one-syllable words that had the same onset or rhyme as the unusual and unfamiliar print 'words'.

For example: if the child could read 'green' with the onset *gr-* (beginning of the word) and 'black' with the rime *-ack* (ending of the word), could the child also read the nonsense word *grack*, which was composed of these two parts? If the child could read *train* with the onset *tr-* and snake with the rime-*ake*, could the child also read the meaningless word "trake"? If the child could read *hat* with the onset *h-* and *new* with the rime *-ew,* could the child read the uncommon word *hew*? And, on the other hand, could the child correctly identify the phonemes when looking at the written word? Which kind of knowledge - word knowledge or letter-sound knowledge - correlated most strongly with (was related most strongly to) the Child's ability to read the unusual words?

Moustafa found that the children's knowledge of letter-sound correspondences could account for 64% of the unusual words they were able to pronounce. Or putting it the other way, "36% of the time the children were able to correctly identify an unusual word, they could not correctly identify the sounds of all the letters and digraphs that constituted the word" (1997:47). However, the children's previous knowledge of words in print accounted for 95% of the unusual words they were able to pronounce correctly. Thus Moustafa's study supports the observation that like adults, children draw upon chunks of known words to read unknown print words. That is, they read new print words by drawing upon the parts of words they already know in print. In general, the more print word the children recognize from the set of real words Moustafa asked them to read, the better able they were to read the unfamiliar print words by making analogies with parts of the familiar print words- whether or not they could identify all the separate phonemes (Weaver 2002: 311).

Mumtaz and Humhreys (2001) also conducted a similar study. They tested the English reading and phonological awareness skills of bilingual (Urdu-English) and monolingual (English) 7-year-old children. They found that the bilingual children had superior phonological awareness and were more skilled at reading regular and nonsense words. They were less adept, however, at reading irregular words, that is, English words with low sound-to-symbol correspondences. Mumtaz and Humphreys believe that Urdu's shallow orthography helped increase the bilingual phonological awareness and general reading skills, but that because of this orthography, their visual reading skills were less developed. This supports the whole language critique of phonics instruction: English orthography is so unphonetic that learning to read phonetically is not very useful.

The top-down model, like bottom-up model, begins with the graphic information and ends with meaning. In order to understand this process, we must understand the nature of graphic input, how language works, and how language is used by the reader; how much meaning depends on the reader's prior learning and experience in the construction of meaning; the perceptual system involved in reading. As we come to see the reader as a user of language, we will understand that reading is a psycholinguistic process, an interaction between thought and language.

Goodman (1976) views reading as a 'sampling, predicting, guessing game'. In this psycholinguistic guessing game, three types of information are used: graphic-phonic information, syntactic and semantic information.

Graphic-phonic information includes: graphic information which consists of letters, spelling patterns and patterns created by the white spaces and punctuation marks. For example, a word or suffix is a graphic pattern while a phrase or sentence is a pattern of patterns; Phonological information which consists of sounds, sound patterns, and pattern of patterns created through intonation; phonic information which comprise the complex set of relationships between the graphic and the phonological representations of the language.

Syntactic information includes: sentence patterns; pattern markers which outline patterns such as function words; inflections which give grammatical information such as ing, ed, s; punctuation-intonation which is the system of markings and spare distribution and the related patterns; transformation rules which are not present but are supplied by the reader in response to what he perceives as its surface structure. These carry him to the deep structure. If he is to recognize and derive meaning from a graphic pattern, he must bring these grammatical rules into the process.

Semantic information includes: prior experiences which the reader brings to play in response to the graphic input; concepts the reader organizes in the meaning he is constructing according to his existing ideas as he reads; vocabulary which helps the reader to sort out his experiences and concepts in relation to words and phrases in the context of what he is reading.

All this information is available to the reader at the same time and is used simultaneously in the reading process. That means, in order to construct meaning from printed materials, the reader's cognitive and language competence plays a major role.

The reader makes important contribution to the reading process. The reading process involves using available language cues selected from perceptual input on the basis of the reader's prediction. Readers guess or predict the text meaning on the basis of minimal textual information and maximum use of existing, activated prior knowledge. Comprehension can not be attained if the reader cannot infer the meaning of various words from the context in which they occur. As the information is processed, decisions about meaning are confirmed, rejected or refined as reading progresses.

Unlike bottom-up processing models, in top-down processing, graphic information is used only to support or reject hypotheses about meaning. Top-down theorists believe that skilled readers go directly from print to meaning because they can obtain meaning without accurate word identification. That means that meaning is gained not from individual words but from the surrounding context. Thus, a reader does not make predictions on the basis of looking at every punctuation mark, word, or sentences.

Meaning (or comprehension) is obtained by using as much information as necessary from graphic-phonic, syntactic, and semantic cue system. These are derived from printed material while other cues are based on the reader's linguistic competence. Research has emphasized the importance of reading on the knowledge or experience that a reader brings to the text. For example, analysis proceeds in a top-down productive manner. Understanding is expectations based. It is only when the expectations are useless or wrong that bottom-up processing begins. The implied suggestion is that reading for meaning would rely heavily on the amount of experience the reader has with words.

The importance of the reader's cognitive and linguistic competence, the prior background knowledge to reading comprehension has deep implication for inexperienced readers. Second language readers may find themselves handicapped in making predictions in English that would lead to understanding texts especially where unfamiliar words exist. This is mainly because they may have only limited scope of prior background knowledge and limited experience with a variety of English words to draw from. Thus, if what a reader reads makes no sense, the reader regresses in an effort to locate the point where the error occurred. Second language readers may be unable to use such self correcting strategies efficiently as they may not be competent English language users.

Since reading involves both bottom-up and top-down processing, a model that synthesizes the two is required which is 'the interactive model'. Rumelhart (1977) theory of reading is based on an interactive model, that is, both from top-down (reader) aspect and the bottom-up (text) aspect, to explain how an efficient reader interacts with the print.

In the interactive models, every component in the reading process can interact with any other component, be it 'higher up' or 'lower down'. Rumelhart's (1977) model incorporates feedback mechanisms that allow knowledge to interact with visual input. In this model a final hypothesis about the text is synthesized from multiple sources interacting continuously and simultaneously. According to him in regard to skilled readers, top-down and bottom-up processing occur simultaneously with comprehension depending on both graphic information and the information in the reader's mind.

Since the top-down and bottom-up modes of processing take place simultaneously, readers need to use their prior knowledge and prior reading experience, apply knowledge of writing conventions, and consider the purpose of reading in order to engage top- down processing. At the same time readers need to recruit their linguistic knowledge and various reading strategies in order to decode the written text through bottom-up processing. It is the effective integration of these processes that leads to the appropriate interpretation and understanding of the written text and creates the interactive reading process.

The top-down processing of a text recruits the reader's background knowledge of both content and text genre, and his expectations and experiences, and applies them to the interpretation of the text, as the reader moves along from one section to the next within the text. This type of processing is easier and more effective when the readers are familiar with the content of the text and it becomes more difficult when such preparatory information is not available.

The purpose of reading is more closely related to the individual needs of the reader and to the personal expectations that he or she has with respect to the given text. Readers need to ask themselves what it is that they want to learn from the text. This could help them think about their long term reading goals. Most of the times, second language learners read texts for immediate results, that is, in order to be able to answer questions from them so as to pass tests. What students want to learn will again be influenced by what they already know and their prior knowledge of the topic to read. If students already know what they want to learn from the text, it will be easy for them to identify the main and supporting ideas, together with details from the text and thus interpret the text with ease. Knowledge of what they want to learn could also help them focus on their goals during the reading process.

The Cognitive Implications of Reading-Theories

The bottom-up model of reading describes the main stages involved in transforming written patterns to meanings and relates the attention of mechanism to processing at each of these stages. According to the model, printed information is transformed into visual phonological and semantic codes. At the visual stage, letter features are changed into letter codes which in turn activate spelling codes and then word codes. When automacity has been achieved, the reader attends immediately to letters, words, and sentences until fluent reading has been attained.

Readers think metacognitively when they consider the implicit meanings in texts; reflect on their own understanding; use multiple strategies to remove blocks that interrupt comprehension. Researchers have discovered that even young children have the ability to evaluate their own comprehension. They can describe and monitor their own comprehension effectively when they talk about and hear their peers descriptions of what they think while they read.

As early as age five, children can initiate metacognitive processes. Such energy positively increases their motivational drive, interest, and reading pleasure. This observation is supported by the theoretical work of Vygotsky (1978). Vygotsky has demonstrated that children begin to mimic other people's thinking when an expert initially assists them in taking responsibility for regulating the metacognitive processes that they use. Such readers begin to see that planning before they read is necessary, and that they should ponder certain things during reading.

Cognitive processes comprise thinking actions that can be conducted without readers placing themselves in the text, that is, readers can sum up, infer, and find evidence without questioning themselves as to how the summary, inference or evidence would differ if they were reading a book from another genre.

Reading is externally guided thinking. Language and thought are interactive in reading but at some point, thought processes leap out and away from the message of the writer. The two statements stress the part the reader has to play in arriving at meaning. For example, Goodman (1968, 1973) places meaning or comprehension at the heart of his top-down model which resulted in his hypothesis testing theory which he terms 'guesses'. Reading according to him is not a passive process as the reader is a language user who interacts with the graphic input in order to yield meaning. In this model, the reader makes use of any previous experience he has had in order to recognize the words and assign meaning to them.

Goodman (1968) places prediction or anticipation into his model. According to him, readers anticipate part of the information which they have not yet read. Readers use their knowledge of semantic relationships in order to anticipate words which come up in the text. Language of the rules of grammar (syntax) enables readers to predict what is to follow. This ability of the reader to anticipate what is coming points to the notion of redundancy of language. For the fluent reader, it is possible to arrive at meaning without identifying individual words or reading every word.

Goodman (1968) has based his study on readers' mistakes (miscues) in reading on this notion of reading but this applies to skilled readers only. Due to this, it is essential to pay attention to the part memory plays in the process of reading.

For Rumelhart's interactive model, a 'feature-extraction' sorts out significant and non-significant letter features (just like the bottom-up model) and these are then deposited into a 'pattern synthesizer' which appears to be a short memory where all kinds of information regarding letter clusters, words, syntactic and semantic cues are stored and evaluated and give meaning to the text read. Rumelhart's model demonstrates the importance of schemata in reading and also the part played by the written text in holding meaning.

Although Goodman in his model stresses that the graphophonemic, syntactic and semantic information is available to the reader simultaneously, the model does not explain the complexity of the human mind. There is no model that fully helps to understand the readers, their self-concept, emotions, and feelings; their view and attitudes to reading. There is no model that explains the kind of experience a reader brings to the text and how meaningful it is for him or her.

Interactive models of the reading process have been found useful for the purpose of this book. This is because it has encompassed the various views of reading in bottom-up and top-down models. Both the schemata theory and interactive models have shown that the role of a reader's prior knowledge and the context for reading play an important role in reading for meaning.

Second language learners may not be exposed to wide vocabulary in English like first language learners and this usually hampers their comprehension of what they read. They therefore require bottom-up considerations in order to complement the top-down processing.

Conclusion

Having summarized the role of vocabulary in reading and comprehension, especially through the "top-down" and "bottom-up" models, the following chapter moves to discuss the role that the metacognitive constructs—memory and perception—play in reading and comprehension.

CHAPTER FOUR

Reading and Comprehension: Cognitive Components

Reading

Recognition involves memory of things past. The interpretation taken at one level is the decoding of words, but it also implies the meaning the reader places on the words or the sentences read. Researchers seem to be at a loss to explain fully as to what stage do reading, memory and perception interact or what actually happens when they come together but they seem to act simultaneously. As Rumelhart (1975) puts it, language is processed simultaneously at different levels. In this parallel processing, phonological, syntactic, semantic, and pragmatic information interact, although it is not clear how.

The process of reading is not very well understood as researchers do not yet know enough about the developed skills of the fluent reader and the end product of the instructional process, as well as the process of acquiring these skills. Reading would not be completely understood until there is an understanding of all the perceptual, cognitive, linguistic, and motivational aspects not just of reading but also of living and learning in general. The purpose of reading is more closely related to the individual needs of the reader and to the personal expectations that the reader has with respect to the text. Different texts may require different combinations of the elements of the reading process. The reason or purpose for reading the text guides the reader in the intensity with which he or she wants to read the text and in the selection of appropriate reading strategies.

Samuels (1983) indicates that researchers do not think of reading as a one way procedure from writer to the reader, with the reader's task being to render a literal interpretation of the text, and in an examination situation, come up with the correct answer. Instead, reading is thought to be an active construction of a text's meaning, proceeding from an interaction between the reader and the writer. The reader must have some abilities to help him understand the text. Memory is one of these abilities.

Memory

Memory is the power that we have to store our experiences, and to bring them into the field of our consciousness some time after the experiences have occurred. An assessment of the strength of the power or quality of this ability can be made on the bases of performance in terms of the quality of the revival or reproduction of what has been learnt and stored up. That means, a good memory must reflect an ideal revival - the reproductive aspect of ideal revival requires the object of past experience to be re-instated as far as possible in the order and manner of their original occurrence.

The term 'memory' (or the process of memorization) can not be viewed merely in terms of reproduction or revival of past experiences or learning. It is quite a complex process which involves factors like learning, retention, recall, and recognition.

Memory is an active system that receives, stores, organizes, alters, and recovers information. The mind is viewed as an information processor. Atkinson and Shiffrin (1969) developed a model which assumes that memory involves the processing of information in three successive stages: sensory memory, short term memory, and long term memory.

There is a difference in the skill required by the reader who is beginning to read and one who has already become a fluent reader. The beginner recognizes words laboriously and has to rely heavily on his or her memory for clues. Her or his eyes scan the print continuously moving backwards and forwards and it is only during the moment of fixation that he or she picks up information. If this information is not helpful, the eyes regress as the reader seeks more clues to help him or her recognize the word. There are no discreet successive stages of sensation, perception, and comprehension that can be marked off. The processes of perception and memory interact in complex ways throughout the succession of stages of visual processing that lead from the original sensory experience to comprehension of text.

Memory and Perception

Mangal (2005) defines perception as 'concrete thinking.' According to him, perception is the simplest form of thinking which involves interpretation of sensation according to one's experience. It is also called concrete thinking as it is carried out on the perception of actual or concrete objects and events.

According to Smith (1971) perception is a 'decision making process'. She stresses the active elements which is part of man's nature in which information is extracted. This does not mean that it is picked up automatically. Extraction depends on the species and its need for survival, developmental maturity, and selective learning. What the reader sees is not clear to the observer but he learns to perceive things in an increasingly effective way for perceptual learning is a growth in differentiation and in efficiency of picking up information.

Perception consists of two levels of analysis: the pre-attentive stage when one becomes aware of the entire features of an object; the focal attentive stage, when analysis by synthesis takes place. What is selected for visual attention depends on the context upon expectancies or the previous experience of the perceiver.

The child first learns distinctive features with little differentiation such as of faces, fruits, trees, and voices (pre-attentive stage), and then later, the representation of things, especially symbolic ones such as letters and printed words. Most children by the age of three years recognize writing as distinct from drawing and will produce linked scribbles to imitate it. It is only later that they learn to distinguish letters. In addition, the child learns the invariants of events which is the base of meaning in written language. It is in the constancy of things around him or her that the child learns structure, structure in relationships between things and events. It is this structure that is important for comprehending spoken and written language.

Perception in language use can not be viewed as a simple series of sound perceptions or word perceptions. It must be understood in relation to the grammatical structure of the language and the structures of the meaning which is being communicated. The size of the perceptual unit is important in gaining fluency in reading. Units act as a filter to incoming information. The reader has to hold in memory the first part of the word or sentence while he scans the rest. Then, the whole word or sentence must be put together for comprehension. The smaller the unit, the greater the burden placed on memory. Skilled readers are able to put more information into each unit.

The way the reader will understand this information will depend on his or her cognitive style, the familiarity of the text, and the language in which it is written. This is dependent upon the schemata readers have built up out of their own experiences which enable them to comprehend what they read.

Memory and Words

One of the changes that are easily noticeable in language that continues throughout a child's life is the acquisition of new vocabulary. Children not only learns new words but learn to use old ones in new ways. For example, they will choose among words with similar meanings the word that best fits the intended communication. As a young child, he uses *big* to describe anything of unusual size. As the child matures, she uses words that more precisely differentiate 'bigness' such as tall, deep, wide, and broad.

The preschool child uses words in a literal sense. As she matures, she learns to use words figuratively. At three or four years, she might be confused by sentences such as "He is a pig", "He eats like a pig", but eventually, the child learns how words are used to create mental images to enhance the strength of a message.

The primary influence of vocabulary growth during the early years of a child's life is spoken language. As the child grows up and learns to understand the written language, another powerful influence emerges–written language. Children who are highly motivated to read, who read often and read fluently, acquire significantly larger vocabularies than children who are less interested in reading and whose skills are not as well developed.

The influence of the written word on vocabulary growth is evidenced in another way. As the child moves through the school years, she acquires words that are less common than base vocabulary words. These words tend to be more abstract and are used to express more complex concepts than earlier words. These words are more often found in written words than they are produced in ordinary conversations.

Vocabulary growth involves more than the acquisition of words, although new words are certainly acquired. Beyond adding words to their vocabulary, learners develop new ways to use words, and they refine the meanings of the established old words and new words in her/his vocabulary. The changes observed in a learner's semantic competencies during the school years can almost be attributed to corresponding maturational changes in his cognitive processing abilities.

As the child moves through the pre-school and school years, her vocabulary and word usage tend to mirror his cognitive shift from concrete to abstract levels. The child learns that words can be placed in categories just as things can be placed in categories. He learns that words can be used in a hierarchical manner such as *big, bigger, Biggest*. He learns that words can be used to facilitate the solving of problems. Learners also learn that words can be used to recall things, people, and events that are not immediate. The ability to remember is dependent on how deeply the learnt words are processed by the learner. Levels of such information processing may range from very shallow to very deep. The greater the depth of processing, the better can the words be remembered.

As further application of levels of processing model, cognitive psycholinguists have extended the levels of processing framework to language comprehension. They have proposed seven levels of processing: acoustic, phonological, syntactic, semantic, referential, thematic and functional. The first three levels are transparent while the fourth level (semantic) is the conscious interpretation of a sentence. Processing of the last three levels depends on context and is likely to result in comprehension provided that there is no ambiguity. The learner has to think deeper and deeper in gaining the comprehension of the text. The levels of processing involve the following principles:

- The greater the processing of the word during learning, or memorization, the more it will be retained and remembered.
- Processing from one level to other levels will be automatic unless attention is focused on a particular level.

It is thus clear that vocabulary acquisition involves more than adding items to ones lexical list. It also involves the sorting of words into categories. As the child grows his vocabulary also grows in size and he understands words differently; as he matures his definitions of words are developed quickly and are superficial, but over the years these definitions are progressively refined. As the child moves through school to adulthood his definitions become specific and precise. The child's initial understanding of words is concrete and is related to immediate contexts. This understanding gradually becomes more abstract until the child has stable and consistent meanings for words that are not dependent on specific contexts.

Acquisition, organization, storage and retrieval of words can not be separated from cognition. The pre-school child's abilities are developing but incomplete. As the child moves from childhood to adolescence to adulthood, he becomes increasingly skilled in using basic strategies for pulling words from his memory.

Chunking is used to retrieve words from memory when words are stored in categories based on their semantic features. The demands on the ability to retrieve words increases as the child's vocabulary grows over the course of language development. When childrens' vocabulary is limited to fifty words their word finding choices are limited and the semantic categories into which the words are stored are limited. When an adult retrieves words from a vocabulary of 80,000 or more words, the task is more complicated. The adult needs to find just the right word to express the right meaning. All children and all adults use chunking in word retrieval, but the chunks change as vocabulary grows.

Vocabulary growth continues throughout a person's lifetime. Through the school years and throughout adulthood, words are added to a person's vocabulary. As one grows older and learns more about words, there is a greater understanding of words and how words relate to one another. By the time a learner is becoming a young adult at the conclusion of high school years, he will understand the meanings of about 80,000 words. If we take into account the changes in meaning by the addition of prefixes and suffixes to root words, the total number of words understood greatly exceeds 80,000 words.

Memory and Comprehension

The pieces of information extracted by the decoding processors from the text are stored in the short-term memory. While there, they enable the reader to make decisions about the text, recognize words while trying to remember what has just been read, and retrieving more information if needed. Getting the text information quickly is very important because the brain has some strict processing time limits. The working memory is quite short; in proficient readers, it lasts about twelve seconds and holds about seven items within that time. If the information is not consciously rehearsed within this period, it is erased and replaced with new items.

Within about twelve seconds, a reader must read a sentence, process its meaning, classify it in cognitive networks where knowledge exists about the same topic, and continue reading. If readers read slowly, they find that they have forgotten the beginning of a sentence by the time they reach the end. That means that all the attention has been taken up by decoding and none is left for the message. If readers must consciously search their memory for value of letters, then their working memory is cluttered by individual letters. When they make mistakes or misread a word, they must start all over again.

Second language readers sometimes read very slowly. Barr (2002) gives an example of learners sampled in Burkina Faso where students learn English as a second language. The students were found to read one word per 2.2 seconds and were correct only 80–87 per cent. At this speed and error rate, the short term memory is overwhelmed. In order to function even marginally, a reader should have 91–97 percent accuracy (Barr 2002: 253). According to Barr, reading performance levels on the basis of accuracy in the United Sates are:

(a) Independent reading 98-100% accuracy.
(b) Instructional 95-97% accuracy–can function with guidance.
(c) Borderline 90-94% accuracy–struggles to sound out words; comprehension is difficult.
(d) Frustration 90% accuracy or less-functions inadequately; uncomfortable with reading.
(e) At the borderline accuracy level, only about 50–74% comprehension questions can be answered correctly.

Given the realities of working memory, reading tests at the end of various study programmes may over-estimate readers' skills. During these tests, learners are given a limited amount of text to process within a given amount of time. But in real life, readers may not have the inclination or time to save material continuously in working memory and may abandon reading. Moreover, learners may pass tests and still be unable to function as literates.

The brain has the means to overcome the narrow limits of the working memory. In order to interpret a text, the reader must become an automatic reader. He must have the ability to perceive the entire words and recognize them within seconds. Words become units and are read very fast regardless of their length. Just like learning to drive a car where the driver does not forget the mechanism involved, reading is one of the many perceptual and motor functions that become automated when a person repeats them. This ability allows the brain to focus on the whole function rather than on single units. (Some drivers find it very difficult to drive on the other side of the road when they transfer to other countries where the traffic rules are different from their country of origin). That is why proficient readers read without straining or with less difficulty.

Beginners read serially, one letter at a time. As they move into automatic reading, they process more letters or entire words 'in parallel' (Logan, 1996). According to Logan, readers who recognize the text and get its meaning in fractions of a second are likely to stay in the parallel mode. When there is difficulty in discriminating letters or understanding words, readers resort to serial processing (for example, in order to read a foreign word such as the name 'Owczarec', which is Polish). Proficient readers use both serial and parallel processing and unconsciously choose the right type to use according to the readability of letters, word difficulty, word length, context, spelling or consistency of the material. Such readers access multiple sources of information in parallel and evaluate them while trying to recognize words. Some sources such as visual feature information are available before other sources, such as semantic content. When sufficient threshold of certainty is reached, a decision is made about what a text says.

The reading skill is retained only after reading becomes automatic. Until the reader has automatized the word in recognition skills, reading may be a laborious process. Slow capacity–draining word recognition uses up the cognition resources that should be allocated to higher–level processes of text integration and comprehension.

Schema and Perception

According to schema theory, the knowledge people have already acquired interacts with new information and helps in the construction of meaning. Schemas are broad concepts which we store in our memories. Concepts are the categories which are formed in order to organize reality and are shaped by culture in which we live, while schemas are structures for reproducing concepts that are stored in memory. They guide the reader's interpretations, inferences, expectations, and attention. They are not merely memories of events but are organized, structured set of summaries of the parts, attributes, and relationships that occur in specific things or events in our world.

Schemata are dependent on the experiences the reader may have and thus become private and personal interpretations of reality. This has great implications for the meaning the reader will find in the material he is reading for schemata will guide both thinking and understanding.

The theory of schema is a theory about knowledge and its central function lies in the interpretation of events, objects, or situations, that is, in the comprehension of what is seen or experienced. The total set of schemata at a particular moment in time constitutes the internal model of the situation. In the case of reading a text, it is a model of the situation depicted by the text.

People do not have a schema for every event, scene or experience. It is not likely that two events will be identical. The human mind takes the knowledge of one set of events and uses this knowledge to cover other similar events. Even in cases where events look similar, the interpretation might be different depending on the reader's experience and interpretation. For example, when readers are given different titles with similar messages, 'A Prisoner Plans his Escape' versus, ' A Wrestler in a Tight Corner', they interpret the two texts quite differently in accordance with the title.

There is a general distinction between content and formal schemata. Formal schemata are structures that represent our knowledge of the different ways in which textual information can be organized. Formal schemata include mental representations of micro–rhetorical structures such as pairing. For example, knowing that an invitation is going to be followed by an acceptance or refusal.

Prior knowledge about language and how it works influence the readers' ability to comprehend what they read about a topic. From experiences, a reader knows that a certain combination of letters represent words (door); a noun will come soon after an article (the boy); that certain words like (because, therefore, next) signal particular relationships (cause, effect, sequence). The reader knows that certain kinds of text such as newspapers, and magazines are structured differently from other kinds of texts, for example, poems, songs, and tongue twisters.

Readers use both formal and content schemata to comprehend a text in three major ways: interpretation, prediction, and hypothesis testing. These processes do not necessarily occur sequentially. Since they are not static, they can be carried out in parallel.

This account of reading constitutes a top–down model. That is, comprehension is seen as primarily the result of the schemata the reader brings to the text. This contrasts the bottom–up model of reading which emphasizes the reader's ability to identify linguistic constituents (sounds/phonemes, lexical items, and sentence) in a text and use these to derive ideational and interpersonal meanings.

Reading is therefore more than a reconstruction of the author's meaning. It is the perception of those meanings within the total context of the relevant experiences of the reader. This is a much more active and demanding process. In this process, the reader is required to engage in critical, imaginative and creative thinking in order to relate what he reads to what he already knows. He also needs to evaluate the new knowledge in terms of the old and the old in terms of the new in order to establish if it fits the meanings that are already present in his mind.

That means that if reading was exclusively top-down, it would be unlikely that any two people would read the same text and arrive at the same general conclusion. It would also mean that readers would unlikely learn anything new from the text if they relied solely on their prior knowledge. Psycholinguists propose a combination of the two theories, that is, bottom-up and top-down. They recommend the interactive model in which the reader brings his prior knowledge to the text but uses the text to reveal the meaning. This would begin at the word recognition level and later extend to the level of sentences and then to a comprehension of the text. The theory of schemata stands at the base of the interactive model as it explains how new information can be integrated with old information which the reader already has.

Therefore, if the reader's previous experience of reading has been positive, the reader tends to have a better attitude towards reading and is motivated to read. Thus, understanding of language conventions as well as prior knowledge about the topic, and the readers' purpose for reading interact to construct meaning of the text. In other words, reading does not stop with understanding; at its fullest, it includes reflecting on what is read, evaluating it, comparing it with what is already known from other readings or from direct experiences, and then applying it.

Language users who have difficulty in processing a text linguistically may not be able to engage effectively in top-down processing. This is the position with second language learners who learn English as a second language and have limited language proficiency. As a result, they usually rely on textual clues provided by the author.

Vocabulary and Reading Performance

Knowledge of word meanings and the ability to access that knowledge efficiently are recognized as important factors in reading comprehension especially as learners' progress to middle school and beyond. Reading serves as ready means by which both first and second language learners can extend their lexicons.

The acquisition of new words takes place incidentally and subconsciously as a result of understanding their meanings in the context. For this acquisition to take place, the learners must consciously notice words in the text. That means, learners need to notice new words when they read; they need to become conscious of them. That indicates that vocabulary acquisition can only take place when learners engage in bottom–up processing in order to fill up the gap in their mental lexicon. The kind of reading that is likely to promote vocabulary learning is reading that utilizes bottom-up processing, induces conscious attention to word form and requires conscious use of inferencing to derive word meanings for the forms attended to. That means that reading is more likely to work for vocabulary acquisition when the reader is submissive. The writer's purpose when writing is to induce the reader to recognize the message implied in the text. If the reader allows himself to be directed by the writer and be content to follow the text like a script, then reading will be an act of submission.

Successful understanding of a text: the ultimate aim of reading; is dependent upon several skills. Some of these have been proposed as, phonological processing ability, word level of the learner and sentence level skill. Attention to gaining meaning at the word level before a learner proceeds to sentence level is crucial and decoding processes can not be ignored when discussing comprehension. Comprehension of a text is logically impossible when a reader can not read the words as the text is basically composed of words.

Readers need to understand the individual words in a text in order for them to be able to understand the complex relationships specified by words in sentences, paragraphs and passages. Readers learn more new words through directed vocabulary instruction as well as in independent reading. When learners activate their schemas through reading more challenging and complex texts, they can learn how to decode new words and expand their vocabulary. In second language learning, formal instruction for vocabulary acquisition and comprehension is beneficial. There is a need for a mixed approach to vocabulary instruction in which basic vocabulary is explicitly taught along with strategies that will allow learners to deal effectively with less frequent vocabulary that they encounter in context so that such vocabulary can be learned when needed.

Psycholinguistic models of reading have placed special emphasis on the reader being able to combine personal knowledge (top-down processing) with textual information (bottom-up processing) in order to get at the meaning of written text. Readers guess the meaning of unfamiliar words by using clues from the text, thus minimizing the use of the dictionaries. As a result, they increase their decoding speed while reading.

Second language readers can be good guessers only when the context provides them with immediate clues for guessing. Insufficient context and a low proficiency level on the part of the learner may lead to mismatches in word analysis and recognition that can cause confusion and misinterpretation of the target text.

In reading comprehension, word decoding alone without understanding the meaning is not enough. In order for comprehension of written text to take place, readers must infer or deduce meaning from the text using the words written by the author. The writer does not infer something, he only implies the message and the reader makes conclusions. That is why knowledge of word meanings is necessary to reading comprehension as it assists inference.

While the meaning of a passage is more than the knowledge of the meanings of words that comprise it, the ability to establish meaning from single printed words is an important component of reading comprehension. For example, an average three year old child can not read a passage because he has not developed the ability to recognize words and their meanings. If a word is not easily recognized, its meaning may not be grasped. Failure to grasp the meaning of the word makes the interpretation of the written text almost impossible.

Relationship between Knowledge of Word Meanings and Comprehension

A number of theories about reading exist in which different parts of the reading process are described. These are, recognizing letters and words, syntactic parsing of sentences, understanding the meaning of words and sentences, and incorporating the meaning of the text in other present knowledge about the same topic.

The theory of Kintsch and Van Dijk (1983) describes the complete reading process from recognizing words until constructing a representation of the meaning of the text. The emphasis of the theory is on understanding the meaning of the text. In 1988 and 1998, Kintsch extended the theory with the so called construction-integration model. According to Van Dijk and Kintsch, when a reader reads a text, an understanding of the text is created in the reader's mind. The process of constructing a situation model is called the 'comprehension process'. They assume that the readers of a text build three different mental representations of the text: a verbatim representation of the text, a semantic representation that describes the meaning of the text, and a situational representation of the situation to which the text refers. The propositional representation consists of a list of propositions that are derived from the text. After reading a complete sentence, this list of propositions is transformed into a network of propositions. If the text is coherent, all forms of the network are connected to each other.

Vocabulary is one area of language that is emphasized in the assessment of young children. It is often used as part of the evaluation to determine readiness to learn for young children. Studies have shown that vocabulary knowledge is correlated and predictive of later reading comprehension in children. Therefore, there is a need for more systematic and planned curricula for vocabulary teaching. This is necessary because educators have primarily relied on childrens' life experiences and as the children get older, reading experiences as the primary means of learning new vocabulary. There should be a strong teacher directed vocabulary curriculum prior to Grade two in order to make a significant impact on reading and learning in the later grades. Teachers should target specific vocabulary which must address both quantitative and qualitative vocabulary development.

Children who enter school with less than average number of vocabulary words may never catch up without purposeful intervention in early childhood. Since teachers are responsible for the education of all children, they should make sure that there is a continuum of developmental levels in every classroom and each reading activity must be reviewed for those children who are developmentally ready for a higher level of enhancement vocabulary. In doing this, teachers should teach all word classes. These include nouns, verbs, adjectives, adverbs, and prepositions. Children with reading delays often lack diversity in their use of word classes.

Thus, vocabulary development should not just emphasize on increasing the number of words a child knows but should also expand the quality and depth in vocabulary usage. In general, nouns usually dominate the vocabulary of a child with reading delay or incompetency. These students often need to increase their understanding and use of verbs, adjectives, adverbs, and prepositions in written texts.

Early difficulty in the acquisition of context-free word identification skills is one of the most reliable indicators of reading disabilities. Deficits in the ability to recognize and manipulate the phonemes of words are believed to disrupt the acquisition of spelling-to sound translation routines that form the basis of early decoding skill development. If these deficits can be eliminated through focused instruction, then the acquisition of automatic word reading skills through successful application of decoding rules can commence. Thus, for children with phonetically based reading disabilities, the initiation of self teaching process and direct teacher instruction have been found to be the mechanism by which increases in decoding skill knowledge are transferred to other reading skills such as word recognition skill, reading fluency, and comprehension.

In a study on word recognition, transfer and reading acquisition, Compton (2005) found that skilled comprehension readers are rapid at word decoding than less skilled readers. He also found that the establishment of decoding skills through structured intervention acted as a boot strapping mechanism to improve reading skills, such as word recognition skill, reading fluency, and comprehension. This is an indication that skilled readers are able to use their skills in reading for meaning rather than for word recognition only. Reading for meaning depends upon vocabulary knowledge, syntactic integration, inferences and other higher order overlapping skills that make demands on the same mechanism responsible for converting the printed code into the language code.

The strong correlation between measures of vocabulary knowledge and reading comprehension is well established. However although there are hypotheses to explain the nature and strength of the relationship, there has been comparatively little research in the context of second language learning to investigate it thoroughly. One question that arises with such research is how to operationalize the construct of vocabulary knowledge. Is it sufficient to estimate the number of words that the learners have some acquaintance with (breadth of knowledge), or is it desirable to measure depth of knowledge as well?

Vocabulary knowledge is one of several components of reading skill that are required as a foundation for learning to read and for continuing to advance reading skill beyond the beginning reading phase. Prior vocabulary research demonstrates correlations with later school success. Vocabulary knowledge shows casual relationships with reading comprehension. There are other aspects such as the reader's behavior, cognitive aspect, and affective aspects that should be considered. In addition, the reader's cultural difference and background knowledge of the content have a great role to play in comprehension.

Word Meanings, Schema, and Reading Comprehension.
The foundation of all education lies in the ability of the child to read and interpret what he has read. This ability requires more than stringing together the meaning of words. It actually requires word recognition. The reader's general schemata or general knowledge structures extends beyond the text and involve the readers familiarity with the overall content of the text (semantic information provided in the paragraph within which the lexical item appears). Semantic information in the same sentence and structural constraints within

the sentence help the reader in decoding the meaning of the paragraph. Researchers have become increasingly aware of the complexities of comprehension itself and have realized that the reading process needs to address the syntax and the semantic issues as well.

But whatever the argument, no one can dispute the significance of the scope of vocabulary knowledge in reading achievement. The assumption is that the more words a learner knows, the larger the learner's vocabulary knowledge is; the larger the learner's vocabulary knowledge, the more he will read printed text with ease.

Recognition of words alone is not a simple task as readers need to pay attention to many kinds of information such as graphic (visual features), orthographic (internal structures) phonographic (sound components) semantic (word meaning), and syntactic (parts of speech).

Lipson (1983) cited in Weaver (2002), showed that children are better readers when they are reading on a familiar topic than when they are reading on an unfamiliar topic. She gave fourth, fifth and sixth grade children attending a Catholic School and fourth, fifth and sixth a Hebrew School two reading passages, one entitled "Bar Mitzuah" and the other entitled "the First Communion". She found that the children attending the Catholic School read faster, recalled more, made fewer miscues and made better inferences in the passage about "the First Communion" which they were familiar with than in the passage about "Bar Mitzuah". Similarly, the children attending the Hebrew School read faster, recalled more, made fewer miscues and made better inferences in the passage about the "Bar Mitzuah" which they were familiar with than in the passage about "the First Communion."

Pearson, Hansen and Gordon (1979) in Weaver (2002) gave a passage about spiders to second grade children who already knew a lot about spiders and to children who knew little about spiders. They found out that the children who knew a lot about spiders before they read the passage were significantly better at answering questions on implicit information in the passage than the children who knew less about spiders before they read the passage. This indicates that prior knowledge plays a role in reading comprehension. The Kenya National Examinations Council Report (2003) points out that learners performed poorly on a comprehension passage which was about socialism and capitalism because the theme of the passage was not accessible to them. The report explains that although the answers to the questions could be found in the passage, the learners seemed to be put off by a lack of familiarity with the subject matter of the passage. The questions required learners to read the passage, understand and respond by selecting the relevant information and also judge the viability of the systems presented in the extract. They gave answers which were not precise and showed a lack of understanding of the issues discussed. This is an indication that learners respond positively to passages which they are familiar with as they can apply their prior knowledge easily

Our schemata depend on a variety of social factors: our cultural, ethnic, social and economic background; our age and educational attainment; our interests and values; expectations from teachers and parents and other factors outside school and throughout our lives. Such factors affect reader's perception of and approach to a reading event, their way of dealing with a particular text and their understanding of it. Reading is not merely a psycholinguistic process involving a transaction between the mind of the reader and the language of the text. Rather, reading is a socio-psycholinguistic process, because the reader-text transaction occurs within situational and social contexts. That means, the activation of schemas and the outcomes of the reader-text transaction is affected by situational and social factors, and a variety of contexts.

Strategies for Reading

Reading strategies help the readers understand what they read. Strategic readers are aware when comprehension fails and know how to change the particular strategy they apply in reading. Reading strategies are like the reader's tools that are used in the transaction to obtain meaning from the text. Hamdy (2002) describes the purposes of reading strategies that improve comprehension as follows:

- To enhance understanding of the content information presented in a text.
- To improve understanding of the organization of information in a text.
- To improve attention and concentration while reading.
- To make reading a more active process.
- To increase personal involvement in the reading material.
- To promote critical thinking and evaluation of reading material.
- To enhance registration and recall of text information in memory.

(Hamdy, 2002:4)

All the issues mentioned above are also important for learning English since reading comprehension is part of learning.

In order to succeed in achieving the purposes of reading, the reader should develop the ability to decode, to infer meaning and to apply his background knowledge. That means the reader should apply the transactional theory of reading in order to achieve this.

Hence, one's ability to infer meanings of unknown words in real time while reading is based on the nature and difficulty of contextual cues, schema memory, and one's ability to process the available information in real time. Based on the above claims, a study was conducted to explore how the amount of contextual cues, cue difficulty and concept familiarity could affect the nature of contextual unknown vocabulary comprehension processes in under graduate nonnative speakers. Results showed that there were qualitative and quantitative differences among subjects in terms of the definitions they provided. The individual performance also varied in terms of the schema memory, and perception. There were also differences between the high and the low performers in terms of quality and the nature of the definitions they provided.

There are three categories of development in reading. These are emergent, developing and independent. Weaver (2002) calls them, effective, efficient, and proficient. Emergent readers are at the beginning of the reading adventure. They have learned that books contain stories, that they can visit these stories as often as they like, that the words will be the same each time they return and that the pictures accompanying the stories help construct and develop meaning. Emergent readers show progressively more interest in trying to read without assistance from others. They are able to discuss what is happening in a story and they can predict what is likely to happen next. They also recognize words in varying context.

Within the transactional model, it is important that books for emergent readers be designed to guide them towards an understanding of what they are reading, rather than focusing on individual words. Students should be made aware that the essence of reading is meaning of the text being read (Hulit and Howard, 2002). As a result, teachers should have these readers' needs and competencies in mind when choosing books for them.

Developing readers in the second category are children who are becoming true readers. At this point, the readers have established the habit of reading for meaning at least in the sense that they understand that meaning is the reading bottom line. Developing readers are encouraged to use their own life experiences as context for what they read. As they process printed text, they are encouraged to take interpretive risks, to make approximations about what words mean. They use text illustrations and their own knowledge of print conventions to sample, to predict and to confirm printed words.

A reader faced with a written text usually goes through a quick sequence of mental questions about the text. During the reader's processing of the text, he moves along a decision making continuum that is basically seeking answers to the questions in his mind. When reading comprehension is effective, there is usually a close match between the readers' expectations and the actual text. Sometimes there are serious mismatches that may lead to difficulty in processing. In such cases the effective reader makes constant adjustments to the text by recruiting background knowledge for top-down processing and by changing strategies to fit bottom-up decoding of the particular text. Such a reader combines top-down and bottom-up techniques in the most efficient way in order to understand the text.

Good readers are not only effective strategy users, but are also effective decoders who successfully employ accurate and automatic bottom-up techniques. They are capable of recognizing words, expressions and phrases quickly and effectively even without reliance on context and therefore consciously use bottom-up strategies mostly for compensation when top-down strategies indicate a mis-match.

Learning English as a Second Language

Readers who learn English as a second language lack a good command of vocabulary knowledge. Although these learners are supposed to have acquired the necessary reading skills especially at secondary school level, most of them lack it. Moreover, at secondary school level there are additional academic and technical vocabularies from specialized subjects such as physics, chemistry, electrical engineering, aviation and biology which the learners were not exposed to in primary schools. Educators can teach these words in paragraphs or longer texts. That is, they should let students read paragraphs in which the targeted words are repeatedly used as it could be very difficult to teach them out of context. However, context is not always helpful for the inference of the meaning of unknown words when reading. While vocabulary can be gained by reading words in their context, some texts give insufficient support or clues for word meaning. Learners need to be made aware that the context itself might be misleading especially if it lacks clues to be exploited to arrive at the meaning and especially if a reader lacks wide vocabulary knowledge.

Guessing word meanings from context represents a poor way to learn vocabulary and a somewhat unreliable way to achieve good comprehension of text. So, sometimes learners might have to use other means for understanding (for example, use dictionaries for meanings of some words); learners can be taught to have cards of both their academic and technical vocabulary. On the cards, they could have their own small paragraphs with the vocabulary used more than once. Expanding learners' vocabulary could increase their linguistic knowledge which in turn could help them with the background necessary for the comprehension of academic texts.

During the reading process, new information is compared all the time with pre-existing knowledge structures stored in the memory. So, background knowledge is important for reading comprehension. If the incoming information is moderately familiar, it is usually easy for the students to understand what they read. There has to be a conflicting situation between the old and the incoming knowledge for learning to take place as the learners will feel challenged by the "misfit" and select it to try to make sense of it. If everything is familiar or if everything is unfamiliar, learners might lose interest and no learning will take place.

Therefore, when the effective reader in the first language may be an efficient intuitive user of the various processing techniques, the second language reader may have to be made aware of these strategies in order to be able to use them consciously whenever linguistic or content deficiencies create difficulties in reading. It is therefore important to encourage the reader to develop metacognitive awareness of the interpretation process and of individual processing strategies. Such metacognitive awareness connects top-down with bottom-up processing.

Teachers of second language learners should realize that what appears to be a problem identifying words may stem from something much deeper: a lack of experience of concepts and the language used to express those concepts in the text. Teachers may need to help certain learners learn to use their prior knowledge including what they have just acquired in the classroom as part of their strategies for making sense of the text. For example, one of the most important pre-reading strategies is activating the learners' prior knowledge on the topic before the actual intensive reading starts.

This could prepare the learners for the comprehension of the text to be read.

Although prior knowledge is activated implicitly throughout the reading process, activities that activate it can be explicit. For example, small group discussions and questions by both the educator and the learner on topics related to that of the text to be read could be formulated and answered. Questions by the educator can foster and guide the learner's search for meaning. In addition, instructional questions guide learners by providing choices that can be acceptable or rejected along the path of making meaning. Thus, background knowledge which is the foundation to comprehension can be formulated by providing questions that guide the learners to the meaning of what they read. Self-questioning by learners could also activate prior knowledge. A reader faced with a written text usually goes through a quick sequence of mental questions: should I read this text? What do I expect to get out of it? What do I know about the writer of the text and the purpose for which it was written?

In most cases readers have good reasons for reading a certain text: curiosity, relevance to personal concerns, pleasure, academic and professional purposes. The reason or purpose for reading the text will guide readers in the intensity with which they want to read the text and in the selection of appropriate reading strategies. Story book reading can be effective in developing vocabulary and can improve reading comprehension and fluency. A research on the effects of story book reading to monolingual English-speaking children reveals several benefits to vocabulary acquisition. Monolinguals acquire new vocabulary from story book reading not only through the use of explanation but also through incidental exposures to new words. The research also found that children with high initial vocabulary levels experience larger gains in new vocabulary than children with low initial vocabulary levels (Senechal, 1997; Reese and Cox, 1999; Robbin and Ehri, 1994).

When learners learn to use detecting clues to meaning from signal words, they learn to integrate these processes into their everyday practice of reading; they learn to let their own imaginations add to the images they form. This creative aspect of comprehension is a crucial element in literal interpretation because it assists readers in understanding the author's intended meaning. This inferencing is guided further by the reader's schemata.

Schema models emphasize the importance of the knowledge a reader brings to the text. The schema theoretical models are based on schema theory which accounts for the acquisition of knowledge and the wider interpretation of text through activation of schemata. Schemata are the networks of information stored in the brain which act as filters for the incoming information. The schema theory has also been described as a cognitive construction which allows the organization of information in long-term memory. The schema theory has been used to account for the role played by prior knowledge of a topic and other experiences in the reading process. Readers activate what they consider to be relevant existing schemata and map incoming information from them. If these schemata are relevant, reading is successful.

The theory emphasizes that the meaning of a text is realized when the reader responds to the text. Readers are the ones who actively construct meaning from texts. The real meaning in a text is what the author intends; the reader has a part to play in the construction of meaning and interpretation of the text. Readers may choose to be 'submissive' or 'assertive'. The submissive readers' interpretation is likely to be the one intended by the writer while the assertive reader with distinct purpose for reading can have a different interpretation from that intended by the author. That means that readers with prior knowledge to a topic or text will be more successful than those with limited prior background knowledge. Socio-linguist and psycholinguists have identified five kinds of students' problems in reading:

1. Learners fail to comprehend if they do not have well developed schemata for a topic. Prior knowledge explains individual differences in comprehension better than measured reading ability (schemata availability).

2. Failure to call into focus prior knowledge at the appropriate time (schemata selection)
3. Failure to maintain schemata when reading. Readers can tend to forget what they are reading about leading to unsuccessful comprehension (schemata maintenance).
4. Over reliance of bottom-up processing. These results in giving extension to graphic features rather than semantic concerns.
5. Over reliance of top-down processing.

The schema theory has been used to account for the role played by the reader's prior knowledge of a topic and other experiences in the reading process. Various kinds of prior knowledge influence readers' ability to comprehend what they read about a topic. The formulators of schema-theoretic view of comprehension have emphasized the importance of prior knowledge (schemata) to the reading process. Reading comprehension involves the construction of ideas out of pre-existing concepts. The role of the background knowledge is summed up by Adams (1980:37) when he states that "comprehension is the use of prior knowledge to create a new knowledge: without prior knowledge, a complex object such as a text is not just difficult to interpret, but meaningless". The reader derives sense and significance from whatever he reads by judging, interpreting or evaluating it against his framework of prior experiences.

It is evident that in a second language learning situation, vocabulary knowledge plays a central role in facilitating reading comprehension especially among inexperienced readers. Comprehension depends on interpreting new knowledge in terms of what readers already know about a topic. Schemata theory asserts that a reader gets more meaning from a text if he has a rich schema or rich background knowledge. The context under which the reading act takes place also plays an important role in facilitating comprehension. Research in this area demonstrates the role of prior knowledge and the context in which reading takes place.

A reader needs knowledge about the content of the passage in order to understand it better. Such knowledge needs to be activated by the reader if it is to be used in accurate understanding. In order to construct the author's message, prior knowledge about the topic is necessary. Sometimes, the reader may construct a slightly different message than the author intended because the reader's background knowledge is different from the writer's but in most cases, the meaning of the context does not change because the reader is guided by the text.

In this schema model, the context under which reading takes place plays an important role in facilitating comprehension. Negotiating of meaning between an author and a reader is a social and cultural act. Reading is therefore to be seen as taking place in context. Rumelhalt (1985:267) cites an example of how this happens: in the sentence "the policeman held up his hand and the car stopped." Readers would have no difficult understanding the sentence yet to do so, it is necessary to know or to infer that the car had a driver and the policeman held up his hand in a signal for the driver to stop because the car does not stop by itself.

When learners read subjects across the curriculum, it is evident that the context under which they read influences their reading comprehension. Readers are faced with a lot of problems as second language learners because their vocabulary knowledge is low and their schemata is not strong because of a lack of exposure to wide reading.

Conclusion

Having thus discussed the cognitive theoretical foundations of reading and comprehension especially in relation to the role of memory, perception, and vocabulary in the process of reading and comprehension, I now move on to discussing various techniques of assessing the efficacy of reading and comprehension. This has been done in the following chapter.

CHAPTER FIVE

Reading and Comprehension: Techniques of Assessment

Approaches of Reading Assessment

The purposes of reading assessment include comparing a learners' progress to that of his or her peers, screening learners for special assistance, measuring an individual's progress over a period of time, diagnosing particular areas of strength or weakness, using information for decisions about instruction, and determining placement within a reading program or special facility. There are many different approaches to reading assessment based upon these differing purposes and on the conception of reading development held by the test designer.

The value of any assessment tool depends on the importance of the quality to be measured, and the capacity of the person to perform the task. Teachers use various methods to assess learners' reading comprehension ability. The method employed depends on what the teacher wishes to test and the theory of reading held. The most widely used techniques for assessment include, Informal Reading Inventory (IRI) Oral Miscue Analysis (OMA), and the Cloze Procedure.

The Informal Reading Inventory (IRI)

An Informal Reading Inventory (IRI) is a series of graded representative selections taken from each reader level in a published reading series and is used as a criterion – referenced test. The authors observe that it can be employed to determine a learner's general level of reading ability as well as yielding diagnostic information.

The Informal Reading Inventory (IRI) provides a mechanism for observing a child's reading process. The short tests help the teacher to place the learner at an appropriate structural level and to determine what books a child can read independently and how difficult an assigned reading can be and still be used as instructional material. There are at least two passages at each reading level. One passage is to be read orally by a learner and one is to be read silently. A learner reads passages of increasing difficulty until the frustration level is reached. Frustration level is that level at which a learner has to struggle considerably with word recognition or comprehension. Based on the learners' word recognition accuracy and comprehension accuracy at various reading levels an instruction reading level is determined.

The informal reading inventory consists of a sight vocabulary test, silent and oral reading passages with comprehension questions and a listening capacity test. The tests are administered on a one to one basis where the learner reads successfully difficult passages while the examiner records errors. Errors typically recorded on word recognition include substitutions of the written word with another, additions, omissions, and alterations to the word sequence. Repetitions, self-corrections, hesitations, missed punctuation marks and mispronunciations due to dialect are not counted as errors.

Both repetitions and self corrections are usually positive signs indicating that a learner is attempting to read for meaning and can self correct a word that does not make meaning.

Although IRI is said to assess a learner's strengths and needs in the areas of word recognition, word meaning, reading strategies, and comprehension, it has been criticized for a number of shortcomings. Pumfrey (1985) argues that the validity of the criteria specifying levels of reading is suspect. The instructional reading level is defined as the level at which students can read with approximately 95 per cent accuracy in word recognition and approximately 75 per cent accuracy in comprehension. Frustration level is defined as the level at which a learner is reading with less than 70 per cent accuracy in comprehension. Spache (1976:33) observes that IRIS is not simple or practical to use because its scoring standards are subjective and probably invalid. Its based reader source is questionable and its testing procedures differ from that used in the research on which it is supposed to be used.

Pumfrey (1985) summarizes some other shortcomings of IRI including the notion that a reader's performance varies with the type of material pressures and that it requires training for one to be able to categorize the reading errors correctly so as to attain accurate scores. It is also time consuming as it is administered on an individual basis. He further notes that framing comprehension questions is a difficult task and that the information elicited by IRI contains an unqualified degree of error. Thus, on the whole, IRI has to be used with caution.

The Oral Reading Miscue Analysis (ORMA)

Another procedure used for assessing reading proficiency is Oral Reading Miscue Analysis (ORMA). Miscues are cases where in reading aloud, the observed response is different from the expected response of the actual word or words on the page. Readers whose utterances deviate from the text may do so because they are concentrating on the meaning and the grammar rather than decoding print to sound. The reader is portrayed as an active seeker of meaning. This is revealed on miscues through reading aloud process. Readers may miscue on any level of language such as graph-phonic, syntactic and semantic.

During reading the reader applies selection, prediction and self-correcting strategies to available linguistic cues in print to reconstruct meaning. Socio-linguists advocate the analysis of miscues, including omissions, as windows on the reading process, as a tool in analyzing and diagnosing how readers make sense of what they struggle to read; omissions are integral to the readers' quest for meaning. Nondeliberate omissions may show the readers' strengths in constructing meaning from the text.

Criticisms leveled against miscue analysis (ORMA) is that the recording and analysis of miscues involves detailed comparisons of observed responses with expected responses which is time consuming and not practical for classroom assessment purposes. The second criticism is that the analysis is subjective and the reasons adduced by the analyst for the miscues are often uninformative. .The analyst is required to decide semantic acceptability of the learners' miscues without any guidance on how to determine certain aspects such as the basic sense of the plot of the text. He has to decide which are the learner's deviation that seriously interferes with the stories sub-plot and distinguish which directions in the learner's oral reading are significant but do not create inconsistencies within the story. The third criticism of the miscue analysis (ORMA) is that they focus on word level information. Moreover, ORMA is limited to early readers in its usefulness and is less useful in enabling a full characteristic and diagnosis of the reading process.

The above criticism suggests that the miscue analysis (ORMA) may not be accurate in measuring reading abilities of learners especially those in secondary school level of learning.

The Cloze Test

The Cloze test is a technique developed by Taylor (1953) and validated by Bormuth (1968). A Cloze test consists of a prose passage from which certain words have been deleted and replaced by underlined gaps of uniform length. That is, a reading passage where every nth word is deleted and the test taker fills in the missing word. Cloze procedure originated as a means of assessing readability of written material. Researchers have demonstrated that there is a relationship between how well people can fill in missing words and other criteria of how well they understand the text. The technique measures the reading ability. Better readers will find texts easier to read than poor readers.

The cloze procedure emphasizes the use of the context surrounding the word to aid the learners in understanding the meaning of the word and of the passage. Thus, the way the reader goes about filling in the gaps is also important. The use of the surrounding context to help the reader guess the missing word is essential to the concept of the cloze procedure as a meaningful way of helping reading in the classroom.

Cloze procedure is essentially a cognitive task. The reader has to reason to construct suggestions to fill in the gaps on the basis of the evidence derived from the context. The completion of meaning based on understanding and meaning is a cognitive task. Cloze tasks involve a range of processes, which are central to reading comprehension. It involves word recognition, use of semantic, syntactic and stylistic features of text to infer or predict.

Cloze procedure can be used to test the development of knowledge of cohesion - the principle by which sentences in a continuous text are related or tied up with one another. It is therefore concluded that cloze format effectively taps into the learners' familiarity with subtle language patterns with a passage and can be a trustworthy measure of comprehension from one sentence to another.

Cloze passages are easy to construct and score unlike IRI and the ORMA. They can also be administered to a large group of learners. The procedure is used widely in the school locally and learners are therefore familiar with its application. The other advantage is that cloze texts adopt an interactive model of the reading process. Its main emphasis is comprehension. Therefore, while setting tests, it is important to consider the three test procedures in order to select the appropriate one that suits the purpose of that particular testing.

The following ten principles concerning comprehension assessment can guide the teacher:

1. Assessments must contain a variety of comprehension experiences, including nonfiction.

2. Effective testing requires that teachers establish goals for what they are assessing and link those goals to learning.
3. Assessments should help learners evaluate themselves. They should be in instruction form. Scores and grades only give the illusion of accuracy and authority.
4. Assessments should be conducted judiciously, with teachers serving as advocates for learner, ensuring their due process.
5. Research in assessment should extend beyond efforts to improve present tests and develop new tests that are more conceptually valid.
6. Diversity should be embraced in comprehension assessment. Informal tests can be culturally based tests to discern learners' multicultural sensitivity.
7. Future comprehension tests must allow for a range of need in students. Some learners have the potential to reveal their inner thoughts accurately; others do not, and still others do not process meaning as they read.
8. Some areas that are worth assessing can be evaluated only through the use of self report instruments (for example, degree of self-questioning employed in whole reading). Interaction between multiple factors-speed, factual/literal recall, vocabulary development, inference accuracy, and metacognitive depth – must be developed.
9. Assessment should be developmentally sensitive and involve sustained reading rather than 'dipstick approaches.' For example, instead of measuring children's ability in one day, using only a few paragraphs or page length passages, tests should continue for several days and be calculated from longer-term engagements.
10. Assessments must be viewed as ongoing and suggestive rather than 'fixed or definitive' (Tierney, 1998:385).

When questions are used to check comprehension and vocabulary, the readers' success depends not only upon their ability to interpret meaning from and ascribe meaning to texts, but also to interpret and answer the questions. In order to be successful, the reader must be at home with the language of the texts and of the questions. What is at stake is the interaction between the reader, the text and the questions used.

Comprehension can not be assessed by measuring one dimension only, that is, literal level. Learners are capable of decoding and making inferences. Most comprehension tests are based on brief paragraphs and often assess learner's background experiences and short term memory of literal facts rather than determining their ability to comprehend a novel piece of text.

All discourse comprehension involves inferences which may be based on textual information (bottom-up information) or on prior knowledge structures (top-down information). Both types of inferences are central to the comprehension process providing the means by which textual structures are related to one another and to a reader's prior knowledge.

Many teachers still ask students to only decode words and give the meaning of those words isolated from the context in which they appear. For example, teachers ask the learners to construct their own sentences using the words selected from the passage. Knowledge of word meaning does not necessarily imply comprehension of text.

Long lists of mental acts do not appear to be very helpful to teachers in providing practice on skills in reading. The following four categories of skill of comprehension can help the teacher:

1. Literal comprehension which does not include thinking.
2. Interpretation, which probes for greater depth than literal comprehension as it is concerned with applying meanings not found in text.
3. Critical reading which includes literal comprehension and interpretation; it goes further than either of these in that the reader evaluates, passes personal judgments on the quality, the value, the accuracy and the truthfulness of what is read.

4. Creative reading which grows out of the others but is totally different. The individual leaves the author's text and goes out on his own beyond the author's text to seek out or express new ideas.

Although literal comprehension is the lowest of the skills, I doubt whether the taxonomies can be used as a description of how comprehension develops. Right from the beginning of pre-school education, teachers should attempt to ask children a wide range of questions not only about their reading but also about stories that are told to them.

Singer (1978) reports a study in which children were taught to ask questions and found that they resisted the narrowing effects of teacher pre-posed questions. They performed better on a comprehension test which consisted of literal, interpretive and general questions than did a control group who answered questions which had been posed by a teacher.

Children are naturally questioners because they are curious and want to know almost everything. Getting learners of all levels to ask relevant questions in a classroom situation of any level is an extension of an ability they already possess.

Conclusion

In the above chapter, I have discussed three major techniques of assessment the efficacy of reading and comprehension, namely, the Informal Reading Inventory (IRI), the Oral Reading Miscue Analysis (ORMA), and the Cloze Test. Having thus established the basic cognitive theoretical foundations of Reading and Comprehension, we are now in a position to see how all this can practically help in the process of teaching and learning within the context of institutional practice. This has been done in the following chapter.

CHAPTER SIX

Reading and Comprehension: Some Practical Applications

Extensive Reading

If readers want to build immediate word recognition and quickness in processing the word mentally, that is, quickly remember a word meaning and link it to its context, which is the sentence in which it is used and also the whole text, they need to engage themselves in extensive reading. This could include reading of texts that are related to the topics to be evaluated in class even though the texts themselves might not be evaluated. While engaged in extensive reading, students could learn to cognitively process as many English words as possible and they could attain the necessary fluency.

Learners' reading speed has to be improved for them to acquire reading comprehension skills. As they read the same text more than once, there is improvement in the number of words that could be read per minute. Regular practice is required before students can become skilled readers. A tremendous amount of text reading would be needed daily if rapid recognition of words in the passage is the aim.

When readers activate their schemas through reading more challenging and complex texts, they can learn how to decode new words and expand their vocabulary. There is a correlation between good reading and extensive vocabulary. According to the National Reading Panel (2000) teaching vocabulary to students increases their comprehension skills. If readers can not understand the individual words in text, they will not be able to understand the complex relationships specified by words in sentences, paragraphs, and passages. Skilled readers learn more new words through directed vocabulary instruction, also when left alone to learn new terms in independent reading and through sharing one another's ideas after reading. As they do this, they learn to apply these new words to their lives.

Comprehension is important during speed reading. Hence, comprehension of the text should be evaluated after speed reading because the ability to read many words per second without understanding the context does not help the student to develop comprehension skill. Quick or automatic word recognition alone does not make for fluent reading. Word recognition without the element of meaning can lead to the tactic known as "word calling" which results in a vocal reproduction of words by some learners. Learning of endless lists of words leads to a lack of interest or to frustration. This in turn takes all the joy out of reading as it decreases student's desire to self-select reading for leisure which in turn diminishes their knowledge about the world.

The above insights could help teachers to elicit comprehension processes separately and collectively. It could also explain to them why a specific thought process would be effective in overcoming a particular confusion or reading difficulty.

When readers experience difficulties in reading the teacher should look for reasons within the reader, within the context in which the learning occurs. Each learner is an individual who brings different experiences to the task of learning to read, but all learners need interesting, motivating and real reading materials which will help them to develop all the necessary skills of reading. All learners require a positive and successful context in which to learn to be proficient readers and increase their speed in reading. Where this is not possible the reader can employ the strategy of guessing the word from the context. This is done by examination of the words and even sentences around, and assessing the part of speech. This will give clues to the meaning of an unknown word and will not hamper the reading speed and efficiency greatly.

The third method of working out the meaning of a word is the surest, but most time consuming and so a little disadvantageous for speed-reading. This is to look up the word in a dictionary. Therefore, the reader should only adopt this method after the first two methods have failed or if the reader wants to check words which he has to know the exact meaning. The reader must make sure that he has chosen the appropriate definition for the context.

Decoding and comprehension strategies are tools that are used during the process of making meaning in a text. Readers use strategic thinking which in turn initiates comprehension process that makes meaning. Critical comprehension processes of fictional text are comprised of self-initiated comprehension processes that transform the literal meaning of words describing characters and events into the readers own mental images and lives.

Readers should learn to use other literal comprehension processes such as predicting meaning from signal words using tilling-the-text thinking and recognizing paragraph functions. As readers integrate these processes into their everyday practice of reading they learn to let their own imaginations add to the images they form. This creative aspect of comprehension is a crucial element in literal interpretation because it assists readers in understanding the authors intended messages. Creative process thinking allows readers to explore all possible knowledge links and choose how they can best tie together new pieces of knowledge as they unfold.

Thus, if readers want to get meaning out of what they read, they must read actively and critically. This involves working out the relationships that exist among the various points made by the author. For example, one part could add information to another, illustrate another, contrast another and provide evidence for another. Learning to read effectively is an important skill which will be required in many situations in life.

A good reader is first and foremost always an interpreter. Reading any piece of written material includes thinking, feeling and understanding the author's meaning and mood. As an interpreter, the role of the reader is to translate printed words into living speech. Three people are always involved in interpretation-the author who wrote the words, the reader who reads and interprets them, and the person who receives the interpretation (the teacher). Readers should recreate for their receiver the thoughts and feelings of the writer as accurately as possible.

Readers should learn that idiomatic expressions are fixed and should not be altered, that is, they can not be substituted for other words. Since they are used extensively in writing and in speech they should learn them. Failure to learn them may prohibit learners from understanding some information that they read. That means they should be familiar with idiomatic English expressions if they want to be competent users of English.

Readers need to realize that context is far more inclusive than they think and should be followed in order to understand the text. They should use their entire personal context of knowledge and experience, their schemas including social and cultural context in order to help them identify words.

They need to use first context before and after the sentences being read, but within the same reading selection. Second they should use context before and after the word being identified, but within the same sentence. Thus the ability of the readers to use everything they know in order to understand unfamiliar words in context enables them to learn new vocabulary through reading. That explains why teachers should not withhold challenging texts from students until they can recognize nearly all the words accurately as such restraint will inhibit their acquisition of new vocabulary. In contrast, extensive reading will enhance vocabulary and thus encourage reading of more complicated texts. Situational, social, and cultural factors also affect readers' perception and approaches to a reading event, their way of dealing with a particular text, and thus understanding of it.

This means that reading is not merely a psycholinguistic process involving a transaction between the mind of the reader and the language of the text. Rather, reading is also a social psycholinguistic process because the reader–text transaction occurs within situational and social contexts. That is, there is a variety of social and situational factors, a variety of contexts, which affect the activation of one's schemas and the outcomes of the reader-text, transaction. In other words, a variety of social and situational factors influence how the person reads and what he understands.

Some Possible Approaches for Teachers and Curriculum Developers

Reading is a way of dealing with everyday problems where printed language is a feasible solution. The largest part of our reading is not recreational but school and work related. Reading always involves two parties, the printed text and the reader. Whenever the teaching of reading occurs, a third party is added to the scene: the teacher. Depending on which party is dominant and which parties are subordinate, three basic teaching/learning approaches can occur. Sadoski (2003:81-84) proposes the following approaches for teaching/ learning and suggests that teachers need to apply all of them at different times when needed.

a) Programme-Controlled Teaching and Learning

In programme-controlled teaching/learning the programme, is dominant and the teacher and the reader are subordinate. When programmes control the teaching/learning situational, the structure of lessons and activities is planned externally and delivered through the teacher to the readers. The teacher and readers work together in following the lessons and activities as planned. An appropriate scope or learning is determined for each grade level and lessons are carefully designed and sequenced to reinforce existing learning and introduce new ones on a schedule. These lessons are delivered through the materials provided for each grade level with various supplements.

This approach is associated with dividing reading into a set of skills to be separately taught and then assembled into the complete reading act. This is done in accordance with the three fundamental competencies: decoding, comprehension, and response.

Decoding is divided into a set of skills including phonic skills, structural analysis skills, sight vocabulary skills, context skills and dictionary or reference skills.

Comprehension is divided into literal skills, inferential or interpretive skills and critical applied or appreciative comprehension skills. Response is usually treated as the final level of comprehension. This approach has great appeal for systematic organized teaching and testing. This allows for considerable individualization of progress: some learners move ahead quickly while others redo skills units until a text criterion is reached. In this programme teachers should have a human concern for their students' individual differences and problems so that their teaching does not become remote and technical.

b) Teacher-Controlled Teaching and Learning

In this approach, the teacher is dominant and the programme and the reader are subordinate. Teachers determine the reading and conditions according to their professional training, experience and judgment. Programmes and materials are used according to those determinations and readers are subject to those determinations. If the teacher decides to deliver one or more selected programmes or coordinated parts of selected programmes, using the specific directions supplied, the teaching resembles instruction. If the teacher works co-operatively with readers in teaching according to their needs or interests using methods and materials that are largely student-centered, the situation resembles education.

Teachers usually selectively combine different methods and materials in their own individual ways. For example, the teacher may instruct students in phonics, structural analysis, context clues and so on. On other days, the students may read self-selected books in order to build fluency, increase appreciation, pursue interest, solve problems and interpret reading skills. In other cases, teachers may invent methods and materials of their own. This may include selecting or even writing texts across content areas and inventing projects to ensure the comprehension of those texts.

c) Reader-Controlled Teaching and Learning
In this approach, the reader is dominant and the teacher and the programme are subordinate. Here, the readers take the lead and teachers and text programmes are used as resources for the readers' learning requirements. The teacher gives the guidance, direction, and assistance. Knowledge and skill are developed more from within. Examples include individualized reading, where students self-select books with teacher guidance based on interest, ability, and other factors. Students confer regularly with the teacher to answer questions, clarify misunderstandings, summarize and read orally to check decoding progress and so on. The reading, the teacher needs to combine instruction and education in order to reach effective and cognitive goals.

Teachers should provide guidance and support when it is needed in expanding vocabulary and in comprehension sheets. They should not just provide materials for reading and then wait to evaluate the success in comprehension of the text as has been the trend. The dependence of the development of the learners' thinking efforts in reading relies upon the direction given by the teacher. In reading, learners employ minimal demands imposed on them by the teachers. If the purpose of reading is superficial, so is the thinking and retention of readers. The kinds of facts he recognizes and can report on are all the direct result of the kind of instruction he receives.

Learners will use their strategies and thinking abilities in reading the way they are taught by their teachers to use them. Therefore, students should be taught to be thinking readers all the time. Teachers need to acquire a wide range of vocabulary and an appreciation of all the purposes of reading in order to have a creative approach to vocabulary development. This enthusiasm for words will then be transferred to their students. They should consider all the components of comprehension and the different abilities and the levels of reasoning that go into the understanding of the text. Knowledge of some taxonomies of comprehension will guide the formulation of questions to test the students' comprehension. Testing should be accompanied by teaching comprehension. Learners need to be taught how to approach the questions and instructions.

Therefore, teachers should train learners in reading sessions to make obvious connections between texts and their own experiences and extend the ideas in the text by making inferences. They should learn to generalize about topics in different texts and demonstrate awareness of how authors compose and use literary devices. They should be taught how to judge texts critically and give thorough answers that indicate careful thought. They should be taught different methods of inference, these are, inference of prediction, conclusion, critical analysis of texts, argument with an author and so on. In other words, they should learn to use prior knowledge and information from the text to make predictions and construct hypotheses about larger patterns and possible future events in the text; synthesizing information to create larger patterns of understanding; questioning the text and the author's intentions and planned structure of the text, and making metacognitive decisions about new purposes and strategies to use as they read further.

The Teaching Process

Learners know that proficiency in comprehension will help them build their vocabulary and hence understand different genres and consequently acquire academic knowledge. Thus, learners should be taught how to read from many different nonfictional texts that address specific domains of knowledge before they develop the organizational system of expository texts and the accompanying metacognitive processes. It is important to teach them that recognizing and removing comprehension obstacles is a genre-specific task. When learners use different reading processes, and different genres, their overall comprehension increases. They should be taught to read expository texts with ease and pleasure so as to enjoy reading a wider variety of genres. This increased pleasure in turn motivates them to choose books from a wider spectrum of interest areas. This self-initiated exposure to many types of texts helps them to think more precisely and specifically.

Teachers should be aware that expository texts are presumed to be more difficult than narratives because both their structure and content are less familiar to learners. As a result, such texts present additional comprehension obstacles for struggling readers such as ESL.

Students should be taught how to identify and follow the explicit expository cues and access features without specific instruction in these areas. If they are taught these features, the task of identifying main ideas, distinguishing important from less important facts, noticing inconsistencies, recalling, summarizing information, and monitoring comprehension becomes easy in expository texts.

When comprehension features of expository text are taught, all levels of comprehension namely, literal, inferential and application increase because learners learn how to bridge the inferential gaps that nonfiction writers leave to readers meaning-making processes more accurately. In addition, when learners are taught how to create mental images from nonfiction texts, the resultant pictures are mental representation of realities in their world.

Teaching Learners Vocabulary

Reading is language and language is made of words. Words reflect experiences because readers visualize objects and events thus forming images of the real world. The more experience readers have, the more words they have and the more words they have, the more likely that they will become proficient readers. Since new words emerge from new experiences, teachers should expose readers to extensive reading that cover a variety of world knowledge and new concepts.

Learners should be taught to be self regulated readers. Teachers should guide them through the process of constructing literal and inferential interpretations. They should be taught how to comprehend single sentences as well as interpret meanings between sentences, paragraphs, within a full text and among multiple texts. Successful understanding of a text is dependent upon several skills as discussed in chapter two. Sources of comprehension failure have also been discussed in chapter five. These include, phonological processing difficulties (spelling), word level difficulties, sentence level deficits and higher level deficits such as poor inference ability. Comprehension of a text is logically impossible when a reader can not read the words.

Experience in teaching shows that formal instructions are beneficial and there should be a mixed approach to vocabulary instructions in which basic vocabulary is explicitly taught along with strategies that will allow learners to deal effectively with less frequent vocabulary that they encounter in context so that such vocabulary can be learned when needed. Weak students become challenged by words for which they can not merely guess meanings by using common sense or personal past experiences. Since they have not been taught the textual differences between expository and narrative text, many content area readings are too conceptually dense for them to comprehend. As they have a smaller knowledge base of words they have less developed schemas to apply to new text, which makes the comprehension of these books more difficult.

Teachers should teach students how to activate their schemas through reading more challenging and complex texts so as to learn how to decode new words and expand their vocabulary. Teaching vocabulary to learners increases their comprehension skills. An effective instructional programme includes vocabulary instruction. If readers cannot understand individual words in texts, they will not understand the complex relationship specified by words in sentences, paragraphs and passages.

Learners should be taught how to use descriptive thinking guides to diagram thinking processes as a way to recognize relative levels of importance within sentences, between sentences and within paragraphs. Proficient reading requires coordination of many strategic processes while reading a single sentence. Furthermore, a comprehension process unlocks clues and identifies relationship among words in phrases and clauses. They should be taught to think to the end of the passage so that they can continue to hold the things they do not understand at bay until they accumulate more blocks of meaning and a complete structure of comprehension. Readers should be taught how to link arguments within sentences to subsequent sentences. In the process, they understand that some arguments overlap and involve more than one sentence. Some propositions can be embedded within single sentences that relate to the larger theme conveyed in a paragraph. This knowledge will help readers to develop the flexibility to become textually bound as well as non-textually bound.

Teachers should teach learners to let background knowledge build by learning to follow along in the curriculum, using it as a bridge to support the passage of relevant personal background experiences to mingle with the author's message.

Learners have difficulty learning how to infer, predict and interpret. They should be taught how to dispel their own desires to move material in a certain direction when their interpretation of facts in a text is inconsistent with the author's train of thought.

When readers recognize a text's macro-propositions, generalizations and themes, independent inferring can be engaged. This will guide them to infer the links that an author makes between propositions within sentences as well as implied logical connections between sentences and paragraphs.

Proposals for Teachers as Examiners

Teachers should be aware that assessment reading tasks seldom match natural reading tasks. Effective testing requires that teachers establish goals for what they are assessing and link those goals to learning. Assessment should be developmentally sensitive and involve sustained reading, rather than fixed or definitive. Given the situation, there must be doubts about the validity of drawing conclusions about readers' proficiency in comprehension and vocabulary from their performance on appended assessment tasks. The role of the teacher is to try to match the reader, the text and the reading assessment task. The aim must be to construct questions and exercise in such a way that as far as possible they work the same processes as are demanded by the natural reading task.

The reading assessment situation in second language learning consists of assigning tasks and assessing individual development. Sometimes, these reading tasks are assigned to students without any regard to their comprehension and inference abilities. This approach should be improved. Teachers can not be content to merely provide opportunities to learn and then assess outcomes. They need to engage themselves with new comprehension approaches that not only assess what they have taught about comprehension but also how much they are actively engaged in making meaning. When such measures are available, learners' proficiency in comprehension and vocabulary and their rates of learning can be assessed which are crucial to planning the pace of comprehension instruction.

Thus, good comprehension is not limited to determining an author's message. It also involves going beyond the message and evaluating what has been read. The reader makes judgments about what the author is saying. Learners should be made aware of the importance of assessment especially in today's information age where readers are constantly bombarded in reading situations with information designed to influence them in one way or another. They need to learn to evaluate reading materials so as not to believe everything that they read.

CHAPTER SEVEN

Concluding Remarks

In the foregoing chapters of this book, I have attempted to analyze reading as a complex learning activity in which readers are required to demonstrate control of a number of variables simultaneously. At word level, readers should understand letter formation, sounds of letters, pronunciation of the words and word meanings. At sentence level readers should understand content, format, sentence structure and meanings of the sentences. Beyond the sentence, readers must be able to integrate information in their memory which is in paragraphs and texts even when the author's train of thought is not implied.

Reading the printed word has such strength as a way of sharing ideas and information and communicating stories. As a result, learners need to become good at working with that information in order to construct their own new knowledge. They need to learn how to derive meaning from written language so that they can become independent learners who interact with information adequately. In order to participate fully in school work, examinations and life after school, learners need to become proficient in the language skill of reading.

If teachers are to encourage learners to be proficient readers for information and ideas, it is important that they understand the reading process itself.

Learners have strategies for learning which guide the way they learn. If teachers make learners more aware of the way that they read, and are able to think about their reading style and articulate their thoughts, then they will be better placed to modify their reading style according to their purposes of reading.

Readers need to be taught that the interaction between the reader and the text occurs at different levels of the letter, word, syntax, semantics and interpretation. That is, each of these elements activates a schema by triggering an element. For example, in English, at the letter level, 'q' is always followed by 'u', and in words, one word generates expectations of other particular words that could occur in the same sentence. For example, in English 'neither' is followed by 'nor' and 'either' by 'or'.

At the sentence level, the top-down process means that readers draw their existing grammatical knowledge in order to complete the text without necessarily reading all the words.

At the level of ideas and meaning, readers must use their memory to recall all their word knowledge and experience in order to enlarge the meaning implied in the text.

Furthermore, teachers need to give sympathetic support to learners especially those who learn English as a second language because to most of these learners the process of mastering reading happens under very difficult circumstances as was explained in chapter one.

Teachers should be aware that the causes of reading problems can be very complex and should avoid relying on the notion of seeing all reading problems as within the reader. As was explained in chapter five, some reading difficulties can arise from problems external to the reader such as a lack of background knowledge, the way the text is written and organized, the language used, a lack of a reading culture and environment, and a lack of enough experience and exposure.

Finally, poor teaching can both initiate and maintain reading difficulties for learners. That means teachers should use proper teaching methods that would improve the reading skill on the part of the learners.

In conclusion, learners should note that becoming a good reader takes a long time and involves a lot of reading experience. With help and support from teachers and a great deal of exposure to different kinds of genres, learners eventually become proficient readers.

Appendix One

A Reading and Comprehension Exercise (Level One)

Introduction
The following exercise passages are set from the simplest to the most complex. They will show the reader how students should be guided during testing.

Reading and Comprehension (Time: 40 minutes)

Read the following passage carefully and then answer the questions that follow it.
Chumley was a full-grown chimpanzee, whose owner, a District Officer, was finding the ape's large size rather <u>awkward</u> and he wanted to send him to London Zoo as a present so that he could visit the animal when he was back in England on leave. He wrote asking us if we would mind taking Chumley back with us when we left, and depositing him at his new home in London, and we replied that we would not mind at all. I don't think that either John or myself had the least idea how big Chumley was: I know that I visualized an ape of about three years old, standing about three feet high. I got a <u>rude</u> shock when Chumley moved in.

He arrived in the back of a small van, seated sedately in a huge crate. When the doors were opened and Chumley stepped out with all the ease and self-confidence of a film star, I was considerably shaken, *for standing on his bow legs in a normal slouching chimp position, he came up to my waist, and if he had straightened up, his head would have been on a level with my chest. Owing to bad tooth growth, both sides of his face were swollen out of all proportion, and this gave him a weird pugilistic look. His eyes were small, deep-set and intelligent, the top of his head was nearly bald, owing, I discovered later, to his habit of sitting and rubbing the palms of his hands backwards across his head, an exercise which seemed to afford him much pleasure and which he persisted in until the top of his skull was quite devoid of hair. This was no young chimp as I had expected, but a veteran of about eight or nine years old, fully mature, strong as a powerful man and to judge by his expression, with considerable experience of life. Although he was not exactly a nice chimp to look at (I had seen more handsome), he certainly had a <u>terrific</u> personality: it hit you as soon as you set eyes on him. His little eyes looked at you with great intelligence, and there seemed to be a glitter or ironic laughter in their depths that made one feel uncomfortable.*

He stood on the ground and surveyed his surroundings with a shrewd glance, and then he turned to me and held out one of his soft pink-palmed hands to be shaken, with exactly that bored expression that one sees on the faces of professional hand-shakers. Round his neck was a thick chain, and its length dropped over the tail-board of the lorry and disappeared into the depth of his crate. With an animal of less personality than Chumley this would have been a sign of subjugation, of his captivity. But Chumley wore the chain with the superb air of a Lord Mayor; after shaking my hand so professionally, he turned and proceeded to pull the chain, which measured some fifteen feet out of his crate. He gathered it carefully into the hut as if he owned it.

Thus, in the first few minutes of arrival, Chumley made us feel inferior, and had moved in, not, we felt, because we wanted it, but because he did. I almost felt I ought to apologise for the mess on the table when he walked in. He seated himself in a chair, dropped his chain on the floor, and then looked hopefully at me. It was quite obvious that he expected some sort of refreshment after his tiring journey. I roared out to the kitchen for them to make a cup of tea.

Leaving him sitting in the chair and surveying our humble abode with ill-concealed disgust, I went out to his crate, and in it found a tin plate and a battered tin mug of colossal proportions.

When I returned to the hut bearing these, Chumley <u>brightened</u> considerably and even went so far as to praise me for my intelligence. "Oooooo, ump!" he said, and then crossed his legs and continued his inspection of the hut. I sat down opposite him and produced a packet of cigarettes. As I was selecting one, a long black arm was stretched across the table, and Chumley grunted in delight. Wondering what he would do I handed him a cigarette and to my astonishment he put it carefully in the corner of his mouth. I lit my smoke and handed Chumley the matches thinking that this would fool him. He opened the box, took out a match, struck it, lit the cigarette, threw the matches in his chair inhaling thankfully, and blowing clouds of smoke out of his nose. Obviously he had vices in his <u>make-up</u> of which I had been kept in ignorance.

(Author Unknown)

Part One

Answer questions 1 to 5 by selecting the best of the four choices given after each question. Circle the letter of your choice.

1. In Paragraph 2 the author remarks that, 'Chumley stepped out with all the ease and self-confidence of a film star'. The author meant that
   a. Chumley had been in films before.
   b. Chumley thought that he was going to star in a film now.
   c. Chumley behaved the way many film stars do.
   d. Chumley looked exactly like a famous film star.

2. In Paragraph 2 the author says that Chumley had 'considerable experience of life'. He comes to his conclusion because
   a. Chumley was eight or nine years old.
   b. of the look in Chumley's eyes.

c. he was as strong as a powerful man.
d. he had no hair on the top of his head.

3. Which of the following is false?
   a. Chumley was bored because he had a chain round his neck.
   b. Chumley knew exactly how to shake hands.
   c. Chumley behaved like a professional handshaker.
   d. Chumley only looked as if he was bored.

4. In Paragraph 3 the author says that he left Chumley, 'surveying our humble abode with ill-concealed disgust.' This means that Chumley
   a. was disgusted by the author's humility.
   b. was disgusted by the poor condition of the hut.
   c. was disgusted by the lack of refreshment to greet him.
   d. was so disgusted that he wanted the author to leave him alone.

5. When Chumley says 'Oooooo, umph', he is
   a. Complaining about the dirty condition of the hut.
   b. asking for a cigarette.
   c. praising the author for bringing his mug.
   d. shouting for a cup of tea.

Part Two

Answer question 6 to 10 in complete sentences.

6. Why does the author get a 'rude shock' when Chumley arrives.
   _____
   _____
   _____

7. Did the author regard Chumley as handsome? Give reasons for your conclusion.
   _____

8. What does the author mean when he says that 'Chumley wore the chain with a superb air of a Lord Mayor'?

9. What was it about Chumley that made the author feel inferior?

10. What three things astonished the author most about Chumley?

Part Three

In the passage some words are underlined. Read the sentence in which each occurs and decide which of the four meanings given below is closest to the meaning of the word in the original sentence. Circle the word of your choice.

1. awkward: A. clumsy   B. bad-tempered
             C. difficult   D. unmanageable

2. rude: A. vulgar   B. uneducated
             C. startling   D. impertinent

3. terrific: A. terrifying   B. marvelous
             C. frightened   D. amazed

4. brightened: A. cheered up B. lit up
                C. shone   D. improved

5 make-up: A. pretence   B. character
                C. face   D. cosmetics.

Part Four

Explain the meaning of the following words in italics as used in the passage.

a. Mind

b. Afford

c. Surveyed

d. Roared out

e. Fool

Appendix Two

A Reading and Comprehension Exercise (Level Two)

Reading and Comprehension (Time: 40 minutes)

Read the passage below and answer the questions that follow it.

Two days before the fateful examination began, I was <u>indiscreet</u> enough to fight the principal's son, Samuel. He was a fellow fifth-former with whom, up till then, I had no quarrel at all. He was inclined to be a little overbearing at times; but then a flint needs contact with another flint in order to spark, and I had been forced to develop from the start an easy-going and <u>tolerant disposition</u>.

    I suppose as the examination drew near our nerves became tenser and our tempers shorter. When during a discussion in our classroom about careers, Samuel declared unnecessarily loudly that he believed all persons who came from the North should return to it to find employment. I suddenly felt my anger rising like a column of mercury. I asked him why, in as calm a voice as I could assume; he replied with a sneer by quoting a Sagresan proverb whose meaning was roughly that even a man who does not know where he is going to ought at least to know where he has come from; and the general laughter which greeted it brought my temper to boiling point. I was tall and well built, but so was he: three strides took me to his side, and one blow floored him. By the time the senior prefect succeeded in separating us, Sagresan blood and lokko blood had mingled on the floor. Moreover, as is the custom with us, the fight was as much verbal as physical, and a torrent of abuse directed mainly against the other's families was flowing out of each battered mouth.

We were bloody, sweating, and dusty when it was over, but still only partly through our respective stocks of abuse. Nothing more than a heightened respect each for the other might have come out of the fight had Samuel been a boarder. Unfortunately, for both of us however, he lived very much under his _august father's eye_, and the marks I had succeeded in leaving on his face were too _distinctive_ to be hidden. I prepared for the worst (prepared in spirit, that is, for physical preparations were known to be unavailing at such times). The summons to the Principal's office duly came after lunch that same day.

He was quite impartial, I will say that for him. We were both arched over his desk and inscribed across our rumps with a dozen strokes of a bamboo four-footer. Then we were made to shake hands with each other and sent off for a walk together along the beach and back (this was the principal's usual way of dealing with a pair of fighters, and one which made a bosom friends of them). That thrashing, and the walk which followed gave me the moments of deepest shame I have experienced, and drove home to me the utter _futility_ and wastefulness of making issues of tribal divisions, in a land where so much else required our attention and our energies. Having heard from us how the fight started, the principal might so easily have wasted our time and his, reading us a long patriotic sermon on the essential brotherhood of all the people of Songhai. Such a theme would have made him appear to me a hypocrite and to Samuel a traitor for we both knew only too well that the differences between us were real, if not deep. Instead we were made to share a fellowship of misery and humiliation which linked us together more effectively than any half-believed fiction about cultural or racial ties could have succeeded in doing.

From 'The African' by William Conton

Part One

Answer question 1 to 5 by selecting the best of the four choices given after each question. Circle the letter of your choice.

1. He says he was indiscreet because:
   a. the examination was so near;
   b. he didn't like fighting
   c. Samuel was the principal's son
   d. he was brave enough to challenge Samuel.

2. The two boys were called to the principal because:
   a. Samuel was a boarder;
   b. Samuel informed his father;
   c. the Principal saw Samuel's bruises
   d. the Principal had been informed of the fight by the senior prefect.

3. The outcome of the punishment was:
   a. the two boys realized they were alike;
   b. they were brought together by their common misery;
   c. they found that cultural and tribal differences mattered;
   d. they were made to believe wholeheartedly in cultural and racial unity.

4. Kisimi realizes from the whole experience that:
   a. cultural differences are important;
   b. we are all brothers whatever our background;
   c. it is a waste of time to talk about cultural unity;
   d. it is a waste of time to fight over tribal differences.

5. Which of the following is the most complete summary of the whole passage?
   a. The passage shows how a fair and wise Principal can improve the relationships of his students even if they do have different back-grounds.
   b. Kisimi and Samuel had a fight, the root cause of which was tribal prejudice; they were punished equally by the principal and made to realize the futility of their quarrel;
   c. Kisimi and Samuel fought because their nerves were on the edge just before the examination, and were both punished by the principal, who showed them the importance of brotherly love;
   d. Samuel and his friends humiliated Kisimi over the shortage of jobs in the South; Kisimi fought Samuel and the punishment they received made them realize that such quarrels are a waste of time.

Part Two

Answer question 6 to 10 in complete sentences.

6. Which part of Songhai did Kisimi come from?

7. Why had Kisimi not quarrelled with Samuel before?

8. What was the most effective part of the punishment for Kisimi?

9. What would have made Kisimi consider the principal a hypocrite?

_____

_____

10. What would have made Samuel consider his father a traitor?

_____

_____

Part Three

In the passage some words are underlined. Read the sentence in which each occurs and decide which of the four meanings given below is closest to the meaning of the word in the original sentence. Circle the word of your choice.

1. Indiscreet: A. foolish   B. tactful
                       C. cautious   D. careful.

2. Tolerant disposition: A. short temper
                          B. soft suffering
                          C. calculated understanding
                          D. polite behaviour.

3. August father's eye: A. harsh   B. cruel
                         C. strict   D. cunning.

4. Distinctive: A. displayed   B. obvious
                       C. clear   D. conspicuous.

5. Futility: A. lack of sense   B. lack of time
                       C. lack of purpose D. lack of hope

Part Four

Explain the meaning of the following words in italics as used in the passage.

1. Overbearing

2. mingled

3. Impartial

4. Rumps

5. Humiliation

Appendix Three

A Reading and Comprehension Exercise (Level Three)

Reading and Comprehension (Time: 40 minutes)

Read the passage below and answer the questions that follow it.

Zero hour drew near, and I was escorted to the ringside. There was no turning back now. But I bid myself take courage. Had I not been told that every man in the village would be there? If anything went wrong I would have plenty of support. So, I took off my jacket, made a few preliminary passes, ducked into the ring, and waited. Then the church clock struck twelve, and a great cry went up. At the far end of ring, where the bull-pens were, I saw a couple of men fumble with a padlock, then skip for shelter. The next moment, a young bull came rocketing forth, small and black as a meteor, his sharp heels kicking up high in the air, his stiff gold tail like sparks behind him.

Slowly, holding my jacket like a shield, I stepped forward to meet him. I was warm with cognac and felt no fear. Then the bull turned in a flurry of sand, pulled up, and looked at me. It was only then that l realized that I was alone in the ring. The boys of the village, on whom I had built my pride, not one was there, all were behind the rails, waiting and watching, and here I was alone. The watching bull had lowered his head right down. His two red eyes smoked with moving fires, his tail switched slowly, his black horns stroked the air. Keep still, I said, and move your jacket thus; for bulls are simpletons, they never charge the man, only the moving cape.

Suddenly I felt the <u>glamour</u> of being there, with the encircling crowd, electric and still, and we drawing their eyes like two poles in a magnetic field. So I stood my ground and moved the jacket slowly, inviting the bull to charge. He watched <u>slyly</u>, lowered his head still further, blew with his rosy nostrils in the sand and pawed the ground delicately with his hoof. Then, in a rush, he made up his mind. With a snort of pleasurable anger he charged me across the ring, <u>jauntily</u> as a tug in bucking water. Nearer and nearer he came, kicking up the sand like spray. I kept my feet together and moved the jacket slowly to the right. Then something terrible went wrong. For at the last moment, instead of following the cape, he turned sharply, rolling his eyes, and caught me head-on with his hard, black skull.

I remember being conscious of no pain at all, only of the high, excited screams of the women and of a sense of utter surprise and let-down. This was not at all what was supposed to have happened. Somebody wasn't playing the game. Instinctively I grasped his horns, like the handle-bars of a cycle, and hung there grimly, while he carried me across the ring, bounced me a couple of times on his cranium, and then dropped me in a heap on the sand.

He left me where I fell and trotted arrogantly away. So I picked myself up, retrieved my tattered jacket, and turned to face him again. The sun shone blue on his steaming flanks. I heard the dry, excited chatter of the crowd. I heard the cries of my two companions urging me to get out of it quick. But I could not, there were faces to be saved. Besides I was feeling cross; that first toss had been a mistake, a miscalculation, but it would not happen again.

So, I stamped my foot and shouted (though not very loud) and the bull turned and looked at me again, rather <u>disdainfully</u>, and flicked his tail, and did nothing. This was even more embarrassing. So, croaking, I raised my voice and began to jump up and down; and at last the beast obliged. It was all over very quickly. He came at me head down, very fast: I made great play with my cape; but this time with <u>impudent</u> humour, he ignored it altogether, caught me fair and square between the horns and tossed me right across the ring.

Fortunately he was a pacific bull, content to teach his own wry lessons in his own way, so again he turned aside and let me lie.

By that time there was nothing I wanted to do so much as crawl away and hide. But having picked myself up, and regained my breath and examined my battered bones, I saw that the bull was now busy entertaining the crowd by chasing two men who had at last come to my aid. So I allowed myself one final gesture. Sidling up behind him, while he was friskily engaged with the other two, I tried to slap him on the rump. But he saw me coming and turned on me with a roar. I had had enough, I turned and fled. I felt his hot breath on my heels, I readied myself for his tearing horns. I ran without once looking back, and dived over the barrier at last – to find a small boy, chewing nuts, who remarked: 'You needn't have run so hard you know. He hasn't been chasing you. He's gone home.'

Part One

Answer question 1 to 5 by selecting the best of the four choices given after each question. Circle the letter of your choice.

1. The author is prepared to fight the bull:
   a. because everybody in the village would be there.
   b. Because if anything went wrong there were plenty of people to help.
   c. Because he did not want to be called a coward.
   d. Because he had done it many times before.

2. By the phrase, "So I took off my jacket, made a few preliminary passes," the author means:
   a. that he waved his coat the way a bull fighter waves his cape.
   b. that he waved his coat to the crowd.
   c. that he bowed to the crowd a few times as a mark of respect.
   d. that he warned up by kicking a football with his friends.

3. Which of the following statements is consistent with what the author says in paragraph 3 and 4?
   a. The author now made no attempts to encourage the bull to charge.
   b. Everything went according to plan when the bull charged.
   c. The bull did not follow the cape as he was supposed to do.
   d. The author felt embarrassed at being the centre of attraction.

4. When the author says he "shouted (though not very loud)" we get the impression:
   a. that he did not wish the crowd to hear him.
   b. that he thought shouting would do no good.
   c. that he did not wish to cry himself hoarse as he had a sore throat.
   d. that he was not so confident as he had been earlier.

5. The small boy's remark is meant:
   a. to make the author feel better.
   b. to make the author feel foolish.
   c. to make the author feel safe.
   d. to make the author feel he had done well.

Part Two

Answer question 6 to10 in complete sentences

6. What made the author feel brave?

7. Why did the author decide to keep still?

A Reading and Comprehension Exercise (Level Three)   113

8. What does the word 'somebody' in paragraph four refer to?
   _____
   _____
   _____

9 "...... there were faces to be saved." What does this remark mean?
   _____
   _____
   _____

10. Why did the author try to slap the bull on the rump?
    _____
    _____
    _____

Part Three

In the passage some words are underlined. Read the sentence in which each occurs and decide which of the four meanings given below is closest to the meaning of the word in the original sentence. Circle the word of your choice.

1. glamour	-	A. greed,	B. urge,
		C. willingness,	D. enchantment.
2. slyly	-	A. deceitfully,	B. cunningly,
		C. happily,	D. noisily.
3. jauntly	-	A. readily,	B. confidently,
		C. powerfully,	D. easily.
4. disdainfully	-	A. rudely,	B. badly.
		C. scornfully,	D. sadly.

5. impudent - A. joyful, B. high,
C. much, D. shameless.

Part Four

Explain the meaning of the following words in italics as used in the passage.

1. *ducked*

2. *fumble*

3. *flurry*

4. *snort*

5. *friskily.*

References

Adams, M. J. (1980). Failures to comprehend and levels of processing in reading. In R. J., Spiro, B. C., Bruce and W. Brewer (eds.). *Theoretical Issues in Reading Comprehension.* New Jersey; Lawrence Erlbanm, Hillsdale.

Aduda, D. (2006). "Alliance Top in K.C.S.E." Nairobi: *The Daily Nation.*

Allison, B., O. Sullivan T., Owen A., Rice J., Rothwell A., and Saunders C. (2001). *Research skills for students.* London: Kogan Pagew Ltd.

Amisi, D. (1997). "Sheng and Vernacular affect performance in English." Nairobi: *Daily Nation*, May 6.

Atkinson, R. C. and Shiffrin, R. M. (1968). Human memory: A proposed system and its control processes. In Kiwispence and J. T. Spence (Eds.), T*he psychology of learning and motivation. Advances of research and theory* (vol. 2). New York: Academic Press.

Babbie, E. (2004). *The Practice of Social Research.* U.S.A., Thomson Wadsworth.

Barr, R., Blachowicz, Katz C. and Kaufman, B. (2002). Sources of comprehension failure. Theoretical perspectives and case study. In C. Cornaldi 2 G. Oakhill (eds.), *Research Explorations into literacy challenges*, 59-79 Mahwah NJ: Erlbaum.

Bless, C., Smith, C. H., Kagee, A. (2006). 4th ed. *Fundamental of Social Research Methods. An African perspective*

Block, C. C., Rodgers. L. L. And Johnson R. B. (2004). *Comprehension Process Instruction*. New York: The Guilford Press.

Campbell, R. & Sais, E. (1995). Accelerated metalinguistic phonological awareness of bilingual children. *British Journal of developmental psychology* 13, 61 - 68.

Compton, D. L. (2005). Putting Transfer back on Trial: Modeling Individual Differences in the Transfer of Decoding–Skill Gains to other Aspects of Reading Acquisition. *Journal of Educational Psychology* 97: No 1 55-67.

Daily Nation (1991, 2001, 2000, 2002, 2005).Kenya Certificate of Secondary Education Results. Nairobi: *The Daily Nation*.

De Vaus, D. A. (2001). *Research Design in special Research*. London: Sage Publications.

Espelago, D. L., and Holt M. K. (2001). *Bullying and victimization during early adolescence: Peer influences and psychological correlates* (123-142). Binghamton. MY: Haworth Press.

Fraenkel, J. R and Wallen, N. E. (1996). *How to design and Evaluate Research in Education* New York: McGraw-Hill,INC.

Gachathi, P. J. (1976). Report of National Committee on Educational Objectives and Policies. Nairobi: Office of the President.

Gebhard, J. G. (2000). T*eaching English as a foreign or second language*. A teacher Self - Development and Methodology Guide. Michigan, U.S.A.: The University of Michigan Press.

Goodman, K. S. (1976). Behind the eye: What happens in reading. In H. Singer and - R. B. Ruddell (eds.) *Theoretical models and processes of Reading* (259-271) Newark, D.E: International Reading Association.

Grabe, W. (1991). "Current development in second language reading research." Tesol Quarterly 25: (3).

Hamday, A. T. (2002). *General purpose Learning Strategies: Reading comprehension.* U.S.A.: Tora.

Hittleman, D. R. (1983). *Developmental reading*, K-8. Boston: Houghton Mifflin Company.

Hopkins, W. G. (2000). *Quantitative Research. Department of physiology and school of physical education.* University of Otago, Dunedin, New Zealand 9001 Sports Science 4 (1) Sportsci. Org/jour/0001/wghde sign.html.2000 (4318 words).

Hulit, L. M. and Howard, M. R. (2002). *Born to Talk. An introduction to speech on language Development.* Boston: Allyn and Bacon.

Hutchison, T. and Waters, A. (1987). *English for specific Purposes. A learning centred approach.* London: Cambridge University Press.

Kamau, J. W. (1996). The role of Science Teachers in fostering Students' Academic language skills. A case of selected secondary schools of Kikuyu Division, Kiambu District. An unpublished M.Ed. Thesis Nairobi: Kenyatta University.

Kamunge, J. M. (1988). Report of the Presidential working party on Educational and Manpower Training for the next Decade and Beyond.Nairobi: Government Printer.

Kenya Institute of Education (19889-1990). The English syllabus for Secondary schools. Nairobi: K.I.E.

Kenya National Examinations Council. (The year 1993, 2000, 2003, 2005 K.C.S.E.) Candidates performance Report. Nairobi: The Kenya National Examinations Council.

Kenya National Examinations Council. (1997, 2000, 2002, 2005) Kenya National Examinations Council; Regulations and Syllabus Nairobi: Kenya National Examinations Council.

Kintsch, W., and Van Dijk T. A. (1983). *Strategies of discourse comprehension.* New York: Academic Press.

Koech, D. K. (1999). Totally Integrated quality Education and Training: TIQET Report of the commission of inquiry into the education system of Kenya. Nairobi: Government Printer.

LaBerg, D., and Samuels, S. J. (1976). Toward a theory of automatic information processing in reading. In H. Singer and R. B.

Ruddell (eds.). Theoretical models and processes of reading. International Reading Association.

Leedy, A. D., and Ornrod, J. E. (2005). *Practical Research: Planning and Design*. U.S.A., Washington: Pearson Merrill Prentice Hall.

Logan, G. D. & Taylor, S. E. and Etherton J. L. (1996). "Attention in the Acquisition and Expression of Automaticity." *Journal of Experimental Psychology*: Learning memory and cognition 22(3): 620-638.

Mackay, C. B. (1981). The second University in Kenya report of the Presidential working Party. Nairobi: Office of the President.

Melink, E. A. (1972). *The reading curriculum*. London: Open University.

Miheso, A. (2005). "Why K.C.S.E. candidates find the English Paper difficult." Nairobi: *The Daily Nation*.

Muthiani, J. (1984). "Language policy problems in multi-lingual Kenya: of Historical sketch;" A paper prepared for the second international conference on Indian Ocean Studies Perth, Australia.

Muya, W. (1993). "Why varsity graduates are illiterate." Nairobi: *The Daily Nation*, 20th June.

Muya, W. (1996). "English remains a hard nut to crack." Nairobi: *The Daily Nation*.

National Reading Panel (2000). *Progress report to the National Institute on child Health and Human development*, Washington D.C.

Omutsani, O. (1997). "Overcome these and perfect English is yours *The Peoples Digest*, April, 1997 18-24: III Nairobi.

Oyaya, K. (2001)."English, Too, Posts Poor Results" Nairobi: Daily Nation July 2001. *Daily Nation* – Editorial 2003 May.

Parry, K. J. (1987). "Reading in a second culture" in *Research in reading in English as a second language*, ed. J. Devine, P. L. Carrell, and D. Eskey, 59-70 Alexandria, Va.:TESOL.

Perfetti, C. A. and Hogoboam, T. (1975). Relationship between single word decoding and reading comprehension skill. *Journal of Educational Psychology*, 1975, 67, 4, 461-469.

Perfetti, C. A. and Lesgold, A. M.(1979). Coding and comprehension in skilled reading and implication for reading instruction. In L.B. Pesmick and P. Weaver (eds.). *Theory and Practice of Early Reading*. New Jersey: Erlbaum, Hillsdale.

Reaves, C. C. (1992). *Quantitative Research for the behavioral sciences*. New York: John Willy & Sons, Inc.

Reese, E. and Cox, A. (1999). Quality of adult book reading affects children's emergent literacy. *Developmental Psychology*, 35, (1) 20-28, doi: 10. 1037/0012-1649.35.1.20

Robbins, C. and Ehri, L. C. (1994). Reading storybooks to kindergartners helps them learn new vocabulary words. *Journal of Educational Psychology*, 86, 54-64

Rosenblatt, L. M. (1978). *The Reader, the Text, the Poem: The Transactional Theory of the Literary Work*. Carbondale, JL: Southern Illinois University Press.

Rossouw, D, (ed.) (2003). *Intellectual Tools*. Pretoria: Van Schaik.

Rumelhart, D. E. (1975). Notes on a schema for stories in D.G. Bobrow and A. Collins (eds.), representation and understanding: Studies in cognitive science, New York: Academic Press.

Rumelhart, D. E. (1977). Toward(s) an interactive model of reading. In S. Domic (ed) *Attention and performance*. New York: Academic Press.

Rumelhart, D. E. (1985). Towards an interactive model of reading. In H. Singer and R. B. Ruddel (eds.) *Theoretical models and processes of reading* Newark, Delaware: International Reading Association.

Sadoski, M. (2004). *Conceptual foundations of Teaching Reading*. New York: The Guilford Press.

Samuels, S. J. (1983). A cognitive approach to factors influencing reading comprehension. *Journal of Educational Research*. 76, 5, 261-266.

Senechal, M. (1997). The different effect of story book reading on preschoolers acquisition of expressive and receptive vocabulary. *Journal of child language*, 24, 123-138. doi:10.1017/50305000996003005.

Singer, H. (1978). *Active Comprehension: From answering questions to asking questions*. The reading Teacher, 31, 8, 901-907.

Smith, F. (1971). *Understanding Reading. Psycholinguistic analysis of learning to read*. New York: Holt, Rinchart and Winston.

Smith, F. (1988). *Understanding reading: Psycholinguistic analysis of learning to read*. New York: Holt, Rinchart & Winston

Smith, B. (1997). *Through writing to reading. Classroom strategies for supporting literacy*. London: Routledge.

Spache, G. (1976). *Investigating the issues of reading disability*. Boston: Allyn and Bacon.

Stanovich, K. E. (1986). Matthew effects in reading. Some consequences of individual differences in the acquisition of literacy. *Reading Research Quarterly,* 21, 360-406.

Vygotsky, L. S. (1978). *Mind in society*, (M. Cole, V. John Steiner, S. Scribuer, W. Souberman, Trans.) Cambridge: M.A. Harvard University Press. Originally published in 1930.

Vygotsky, L. S. (1986). *Thought and language* (A. Kozuhn, Trans.) Cambridge, M.A: MIT Press (original work published 1934).

Waithaka, J. M. (1993). "English across the curriculum – The Ministry of Education's Position in the proceedings of the conference on "English across the curriculum," The Kenyan context. Nairobi: The British Council, May.

Weaver, C. (2002). Reading Process and Practice. Portsmonth NH: Heinemann.

Index of Personal Names

Adams, M. J., 74
Aduda, D., 6
Allison B., 12
Amisi D., 3
Anderson R. C., 24
Armbruster B. B., 32
Atkinson, R. C., 50

Babbie E., 12
Barr R., 56
Bless C., 12
Block C. C., 21
Bormuth J. R., 80

Compton D. L., 64
Cox A., 72
Campbell R., 32

De Vaus D. A., 12

Ehri L. C., 72
Espelago D. L., 2

Fraenkel J. R, 12

Gebhard J. G., 7, 23
Goetz E. T., 32
Goodman K. S., 39, 41, 45, 46

Hamday, A. T., 67, 68
Hittleman D. R., 21
Hopkins W. G., 12
Hutchinson T., 8
Humhreys G. W., 40

Kamau J. W., 9
Kintsch W., 32, 63

LaBerge D., 35, 36, 37
Leedy A. D., 12
Lesgold, A.M., 32
Logan G. D., 57

Mangal S. K., 51
Melink E. A., 26
Miheso A. 9
Mumtaz S., 40
Muthiani J., 2, 3
Moustafa M., 39, 40
Muya W., 4, 7

Omutsani O., 3
Ormrod J. E., 12

Parry K. J., 23
Pearson D. M., 66
Perfetti C. A., 32
Pumfrey D. P., 78, 79

Reaves C. C., 12
Reese E., 72
Robbin C., 72
Rosenblatt L. M., 22
Rossouw D., 12
Rumelhart D. E., 43, 46, 49, 75

Sais E., 32
Sadoski M., 89
Samuels S. J., 35, 36, 37, 50
Senechal M., 72
Shiffrin, R. M., 50
Singer H., 84
Smith B., 20, 39, 51

Storch S. A., 8

Taylor B., 80

Waithaka J. M., 3, 4
Wallen N. E., 2
Waters A., 8
Weaver C., 20, 21, 33, 34, 39, 40, 66, 69
Whitehurst G. J., 8

Vygotsky L. S., 25, 45
Van Dijk T.A., 63

Zapf Chancery Tertiary Level Publications

A Guide to Academic Writing by **C. B. Peter** (1994)
Africa in the 21st Century by **Eric M. Aseka** (1996)
Women in Development by **Egara Kabaji** (1997)
Introducing Social Science: A Guidebook by **J. H. van Doorne** (2000)
Elementary Statistics by **J. H. van Doorne** (2001)
Iteso Survival Rites on the Birth of Twins by **Festus B. Omusolo** (2001)
The Church in the New Millennium: Three Studies in the Acts of the Apostles by **John Stott** (2002)
Introduction to Philosophy in an African Perspective by **Cletus N. Chukwu** (2002)
Participatory Monitoring and Evaluation by **Francis W. Mulwa and Simon N. Nguluu** (2003)
Applied Ethics and HIV/AIDS in Africa by **Cletus N. Chukwu** (2003)
For God and Humanity: 100 Years of St. Paul's United Theological College Edited by **Emily Onyango** (2003)
Establishing and Managing School Libraries and Resource Centres by **Margaret Makenzi and Raymond Ongus** (2003)
Introduction to the Study of Religion by **Nehemiah Nyaundi** (2003)
A Guest in God's World: Memories of Madagascar by **Patricia McGregor** (2004)
Introduction to Critical Thinking by **J. Kahiga Kiruki** (2004)
Theological Education in Contemporary Africa edited by **GrantLeMarquand and Joseph D. Galgalo** (2004)
Looking Religion in the Eye edited by **Kennedy Onkware** (2004)
Computer Programming: Theory and Practice by **Gerald Injendi** (2005)
Demystifying Participatory Development by **Francis W. Mulwa** (2005)
Music Education in Kenya: A Historical Perspective by **Hellen A. Odwar** (2005)
Into the Sunshine: Integrating HIV/AIDS into Ethics Curriculum Edited by **Charles Klagba and C. B. Peter** (2005)
Integrating HIV/AIDS into Ethics Curriculum: Suggested Modules Edited by **Charles Klagba** (2005)
Dying Voice (An Anthropological Novel) by **Andrew K. Tanui** (2006)
Participatory Learning and Action (PLA): A Guide to Best Practice by **Enoch Harun Opuka** (2006)

Science and Human Values: Essays in Science, Religion, and Modern Ethical Issues edited **by Nehemiah Nyaundi and Kennedy Onkware** (2006)
Understanding Adolescent Behaviour **by Daniel Kasomo** (2006)
Students' Handbook for Guidance and Counselling **by Daniel Kasomo** (2007)
BusinessOrganization and Management: Questions and Answers **by Musa O. Nyakora** (2007)
Auditing Priniples: A Stuents' Handbook **by Musa O. Nyakora** (2007)
The Concept of Botho and HIV/AIDS in Botswana edite **by Joseph B. R. Gaie and Sana K. MMolai** (2007)
Captive of Fate: A Novel **by Ketty Arucy** (2007)
A Guide to Ethics **by Joseph Njino** (2008)
Pastoral Theology: Rediscovering African Models and Methods **by Ndung'u John Brown Ikenye** (2009)
The Royal Son: Balancing Barthian and African Christologies **by Zablon Bundi Mutongu** (2009)
AIDS, Sexuality, and Gender: Experiencing of Women in Kenyan Universities **by Nyokabi Kamau** (2009)
Modern Facilitation and Training Methodology: A Guide to Best Practice in Africa **by Frederick Chelule** (2009)
How to Write a Winning Thesis **by Simon Kang'ethe et al** (2009)
Absolute Power and Other Stories **by Ambrose Rotich Keitany** (2009)
Y'sdom in Africa: A Personal Journey **by Stanley Kinyeki** (2010)
Abortion and Morality Debate in Africa: A Philosophical Enquiry **by George Kegode** (2010)
The Holy Spirit as Liberator: A Study of Luke 4: 14-30 **by Joseph Koech** (2010)
Biblical Studies, Theology, Religion and Philosophy: An Introduction for African Universities, **Gen. Ed. James N. Amanze** (2010)
Modeling for Servant-Leaders in Africa: Lessons from St. Paul **by Ndung'u John Brown Ikenye** (2010)
HIV & AIDS, Communication and Secondary Education in Kenya **by Ndeti Ndati** (2011)
Disability, Society and Theology: Voices from Africa **by Samuel Kabue et al** (2011)
If You Have No Voice Just Sing!: Narratives of Women's Lives and Theological Education at St. Paul's University **by Esther Mombo And Heleen Joziasse** (2011)

Mutira Mission: An African Church Comes of Age in Kirinyaga, Kenya (1912-2012) **by Julius Gathogo** (2011)
The Bible and African Culture: Mapping Transactional Inroads **by Humphrey Waweru** (2011)
Karl Jaspers' Philosophy of Existence: Insights for Out Time **by Cletus N. Chukwu** (2011)
Diet of Worms: Quality of Catering in Kenyan Prisons **by Jacqueline Cheptekkeny Korir** (2011)
Our Father! An Indian Christian Prays the Lord's Prayer **by C. B. Peter** (2011)
African Christianity: The Stranger Within **by Joseph D. Galgalo** (2012)
A Handbook of African Church History **by Medard Rugyendo** (2012)
Project Planning and Management: A Kenyan Experience **by Zablon Bundi Mutongu and Lily Wanjiku Njanja** (2012)
Reading and Comprehension in the African Context: A Cognative Enquiry **by Agnes Wanja Kibui** (2012)

******

Worldwide Distributors of Zapf Chancery Publications

AFRICAN BOOKS COLLECTIVE (www.africanbookscollective.com)
PO Box 721
Oxford OX1 9EN
UK Tel: +44 (0) 1865 58 9756
Fax: +44 (0) 1865 412 341
US Tel: +1 415 644 5108
Customer Services please email orders@africanbookscollective.com
Marketing and Production Justin Cox
justin.cox@africanbookscollective.com
US Customer Assistance Carolina Bruno
carolina.bruno@africanbookscollective.com

www.ingramcontent.com/pod-product-compliance
Lightning Source LLC
Chambersburg PA
CBHW020618300426
44113CB00007B/688